LIVE IN YOUR WHEEL HOUSE

LIVE IN YOUR WHEEL HOUSE

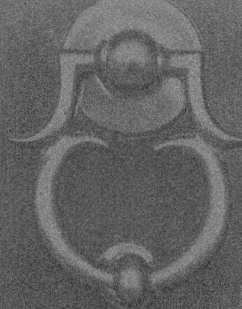

An Empowering
Guide to
Stay, Go, or Reno

Kim Costa

Story BUILDERS PRESS

Live in Your Wheel House: An Empowering Guide to Stay, Go, or Reno
Copyright © 2026 Kim Costa

No part of this book may be reproduced or transmitted in any form or by any means, electronic or mechanical, including photocopying and recording, or by any information storage or retrieval system, except as may be expressly permitted by the Copyright Act of 1976 or in writing from the publisher. Requests for permission should be addressed to *storybuilderspress@gmail.com*.

Disclaimer: Stories in this book are inspired by real-life experiences, but all names and details have been changed to protect privacy. Any resemblance to real people is coincidental. This book is for informational purposes only and is not financial, medical, or psychological advice. Please seek a qualified professional for any financial, personal health, or mental health concerns.

Published by StoryBuilders Press
Hardcover: 979-8-89833-058-3
Paperback: 979-8-89833-059-0
eBook: 979-8-89833-060-6
Audiobook: 979-8-89833-061-3

To my mom, who taught me that a home is made warm not by its walls but by the love within them. You and Dad always showed me what welcome truly means.

To Lauren and Zack. Being your mom is the greatest honor and privilege of my life. You inspire me every day to live more authentically and love more fully.

And to Rocky. Life is simply better with you in it. I love the home and the life we make together, and I'm so thankful for you.

Contents

Introduction: Live in Your Wheel House *1*

Part 1: Clarity Farm: A Personal Case Study *11*
    Chapter 1: Seeking Clarity *13*
    Chapter 2: Hard-Hitting Clarity *17*
    Chapter 3: Clarity Silenced *21*
    Chapter 4: For Clarity's Sake *25*

Part 2: A Home for Your Soul: Fundamental Theories of the Wheel House Process *31*
    Chapter 5: My True Self: Home Transformation *33*
    Chapter 6: The State of Happiness at Home *37*
    Chapter 7: The Home as a Representation of Self *41*
    Chapter 8: Maslow's Hierarchy in Your Home *49*
    Chapter 9: The Wheel of Life *55*
    Chapter 10: The Wheel House Method: A Complete Process *59*

Part 3: The Wheel House Foundation: The 4Ms *75*
    Chapter 11: My Self *77*
    Chapter 12: Mastery *81*
    Chapter 13: Mission *87*
    Chapter 14: Mate(s) *91*

Part 4: The Wheel House Assessment: Creating Your Ideal Living Environment *99*
    Chapter 15: Health *105*
    Chapter 16: Career *117*
    Chapter 17: Fun and Leisure *129*
    Chapter 18: Family and Friends *141*
    Chapter 19: Spirituality *153*
    Chapter 20: Romance *165*
    Chapter 21: Environment *177*
    Chapter 22: Finance *189*

Part 5: Wheel House Assessment Outcomes *201*
    Chapter 23: Interpreting Your Wheel House Score *203*
    Chapter 24: Stay, Go, or Reno? *207*

Conclusion: The Wheel House Hall of Fame *213*
Afterword: Overcoming Barriers to Self *219*
Acknowledgments *225*
About the Author *227*
Notes *229*

Introduction

LIVE IN YOUR WHEEL HOUSE

Welcome to a new stage of your life—one where you embrace your innate nature, gifts, and unspoken desires. You will learn how to create an environment and lifestyle that empower success in all areas of your life while attracting the people and opportunities that support you and your mission. This is what I call living in your Wheel House.

I developed the Wheel House process over the past decade of reinventing myself mid-life. I changed everything. Not long ago I was living a false life, ignoring my gifts, working at the wrong job, residing in the wrong house, involved in the wrong relationship, and even pursuing the wrong hobbies. Very few elements of my lifestyle supported the real me.

Despite a glossy exterior, my life felt empty and misaligned. For decades I had done what everyone else needed me to do, not what I wanted to do. Over the years I learned to develop a false self to adapt to my surroundings like a chameleon. But I always dreamed of a different life where I could be authentic and celebrated for my creative and intuitive gifts. I secretly desired a more genuine, centered way of life.

As my life changed, I realized that my home needed to change as well. And when my home changed, I found that my life also changed, and you will likely find that to be true as well. Embracing evolution and making changes to your home and lifestyle need to go hand in hand. Part of living your best life is letting go of old ways that no longer serve you—or perhaps never did.

Growing up in an upper-middle-class suburb of Atlanta, I used to sit at the dinner table with my parents who were both human resource professionals. They discussed the people they hired and why they were perfect for the job, or why they had to fire someone because they didn't work out. They said the job was just "not in their wheelhouse."

We had a bookcase in our family room where my father kept books he enjoyed. Titles such as *In Search of Excellence*, *The Seven Habits of Highly Effective People*, and *What Color Is Your Parachute?* were the backdrop of my growing-up years. They were all books that focus on practical ways to identify your strengths and maximize your potential. I'd often pick up one that caught my eye and devour it.

Often these books focused on maximizing people's unique personalities and potential. My father was known for his humor, his individualized care for people, his state-of-the-art personality testing, and the best wellness programs and positive work environments he created for his employees. When someone came to his office and asked for help, he always said yes first and then asked, "Now, what can I do for you?"

Not to be outdone, my mother followed him into the human resource field after being a homemaker and teacher for many years. During the recession in the 1970s, she transitioned from being a part-time school teacher and full-time mom to a secretary, helping pay the bills after my two oldest brothers entered college. The company must have recognized her people skills and how smart she was because she was promoted to human resources manager within a few years. She often traveled to satellite offices to fix personnel problems and resolve disputes, becoming exposed to a wide variety of people we might not usually have run into in our little bubble of a town.

Growing up with two caring and generous parents whose focus was most often on people skills and maximizing potential gave me great insight. Here's what I learned from them:

- People are people on the inside, no matter how they look on the outside or where they come from.
- Not everyone is cut out for a particular job or lifestyle. People are born with specific skills, interests, personalities, and proclivities.
- Societal and family pressures sometimes lead a person to choose a path not naturally suited to them.
- Sometimes people's home lives and backgrounds interfere with their ability to do a good job and reach their potential. Offering resources to help them spiritually, mentally, health-wise, and educationally was a mission that both of my parents took seriously.
- People aren't all given the same opportunities to succeed in life. Some grow up with trauma and lack access to schooling, and some face discrimination. Some are encouraged to be something other than who they are innately, and they struggle to find their authenticity and calling. Later in life they may wonder why they are unhappy.

By all accounts, I grew up living a charmed life. I excelled in school, lived in a safe community, had access to quality education, attended a local church with my family, had plenty of extracurricular activities, and had lots of friends. And yet somehow, even with all my advantages, I ended up living an inauthentic life.

Through my continued love of learning and interest in what makes people tick, I learned the following along the journey to reclaim my true self:

- Unresolved trauma can wreak havoc. If heartbreak or lingering fear goes unrecognized or undealt with, it lives in the mind and the body until it is released and tamed. Trauma can also be passed on generationally. Unresolved trauma is a barrier to living an authentic life.
- Everyone is born with a unique personality. Just as there are systems and a rhyme and reason to our universe, so there are to the way people within it are made. If we follow what comes to us naturally, we can eliminate a lot of pain and failure.
- Throughout childhood, people from every walk of life adapt to their circumstances and learn specific ways to cope with hardships. These coping mechanisms not only affect their personality but become an integral part of it alongside the original way they were made.
- Every personality has a dark side, and we can fall into it if we are unhealthy, disingenuous, traumatized, unrecognized, unsupported, or ill.
- There is always resistance to becoming our highest, authentic self. It can be sabotage from others, ourselves, or some other adversity. To paraphrase author Steven

Pressfield, we should expect it. And once we commit to our calling, aid will come. Like a spinning wheel, we will gain momentum when we align with our true self and calling.

- Our state of self-care is directly proportional to the state of our environment.
- There is a specific set of environmental criteria that helps every unique individual meet their highest potential.
- Our society is growing increasingly distant from authenticity and health of the mind, body, and soul. The health of our society depends on the health of each individual, each home, and each community.

I created the Wheel House Assessment tool that I detail in this book through my own learning process as I transitioned from a long career as an accountant to become a real estate agent and life design expert, from being married to the wrong person to being married to my soulmate, from living as a human *doing* to becoming an authentic human *being*, and from not being comfortable in my own home to developing a lifestyle and home that fit me perfectly. I later tweaked the Wheel House Method by helping many clients find and create their perfect homes and lifestyles.

The goal of creating the Wheel House Method is to help as many people as possible create a home that aligns perfectly with their true self and their soul, and then to maximize the potential of that lifestyle so they can help others with their gifts.

My mission is to bring this process to as many people as possible so they don't waste precious time living inauthentically and unhappily. While the initial work will be for you to establish who you are and what you are called to do, the bulk of this process is meant to create a unique environment that reinforces and supports your best self. In turn, as your best self in an environment that supports your life's mission, you will have a positive impact on society as a whole.

In **Part 1**, I explain what led to the development of the Wheel House Method.

In **Part 2**, I'll give some theoretical background on which the Wheel House Method is based, combining ideas from some of the best thinkers of our time.

In **Part 3**, we'll look at the foundation of living—the 4Ms. Like the foundation of a house, it provides structure and support for living an aligned and joyful life.

Part 4 gets right to the meat of the Wheel House Assessment. You'll examine eight areas of your life through research findings, case studies, and a series of probing questions you might consider when analyzing your current and ideal living environments.

In **Part 5**, we'll sum it all up.

If you are just beginning to consider a change, if you are feeling some discomfort or are curious about maximizing your home's potential, take your time reading the background information in Parts 1, 2, and 3 so you have a complete understanding of the supporting theories and the process. The examples are meant to pique your interest and spark ideas for living your most whole life.

But if you're short on time, start in Part 4 and take the assessment to obtain your results quickly. For example, suppose it's Tuesday and you, the homebuyer, have started reading this book with the goal of touring homes for sale with your real estate agent on Saturday. It will save both you and your agent a significant amount of time, money, and potential heartbreak if you have your Wheel House Assessment results first.

Also, you may not be ready to change your home yet because of some underlying, more serious problems. We'll talk about these barriers in the Afterword. Not everyone can start the Wheel House Assessment right away, but I hope this book inspires you to map out what your dream life might look like. It is possible. And when you're ready to roll, I'll be in your corner.

Being your most authentic self starts and ends at home—*your* home. It's in your own Wheel House.

Part 1

CLARITY FARM—

A Personal Case Study

Chapter 1

SEEKING CLARITY

Let me take you back to the era of my story when transforming my home was my path to transforming my life. I was about a decade into my marriage to my then-husband, my high-school sweetheart, raising two very much-loved preschool children. When someone in the immediate family went through a contentious divorce settlement, I had to leave my coveted sales job at Xerox, manage a newly acquired family-run residential construction business, and assume the financial responsibilities.

It was a stressful and overwhelming time. The daily turmoil from disgruntled family members who lived nearby and the demands of our newly acquired business were taking a toll on our family life. So we decided to move as far away as possible while still managing our thriving business.

In pursuit of a peaceful home away from the noise, I spent over a year looking for the perfect piece of land to build our family's peaceful escape from the all-consuming yet lucrative family construction business, the traffic, and the fast pace of big-city Atlanta.

In those days before GPS, the thick, frayed Metro Atlanta map book I kept in the pocket behind the driver's seat of my white Suburban was all marked up with streets circled in red to highlight where I thought our future getaway farm could be. Every week while my kids were at preschool, I searched high and low down country back roads for unlisted properties.

On one fateful trip, I ventured down Clarity Road. The tree-canopied, dusty, gravel drive wound downhill and spanned two counties. It started at the very northern tip of a populated county that also housed the big city of Atlanta.

The other end landed in a more northerly county that heralded back to a quieter, gentler time and the agricultural era that thrived there.

My Suburban crossed an old, one-lane bridge over the pristine Little River that divided the two counties. Beyond the bridge was four-board horse fencing, grass as green as a four-leaf clover, and a beautiful valley. It was as if I had gone back in time through a hidden portal a thousand miles away from the bustling city. I slowed down to take it all in and wondered, *Who owns this beautiful property?*

About 50 yards past the bridge on the left side, a faded "For Sale by Owner" sign with a 404 area code appeared on the vine-covered, four-board fence. I wrote down the barely legible number so I could call it when I returned home. I envisioned the perfect building site on a wooded hill above the pastures and the valley floor—a potential slice of heaven.

After picking up the kids, I called the number to arrange access to the property behind the padlocked gate. My heart grew bigger with anticipation when a pleasant voice with a southern gentleman's drawl answered. I hit it off with the owner, a congenial fellow whose Atlanta-based family owned much of the surrounding property, and I arranged for my then-husband and I to meet him there on Clarity Road.

The view from the perch on the hill above the valley was even more beautiful than I had imagined. We soon purchased the property, selected the best building site, and began developing the land and designing our custom home. Over the next year, Clarity Farm turned from a vision into our family's dream home.

Chapter 2

HARD-HITTING CLARITY

A few years later, the day after Christmas in 2001, I arranged for a dressage lesson to learn how to control my new horse, Sergeant. My beloved prior horse, Phoenix, had turned up lame earlier that fall and was going to be donated to a hippotherapy program that uses horseback riding as physical and emotional therapy for people with disabilities.

My goal with Sergeant was to join my then-husband and daughter in a fox-hunting expedition, an endeavor I was not aligned with and more than a little nervous about. I've always been a golfer at heart, and I prefer my feet on the ground.

But that day, just like many others, I went along with it. I donned my Christmas gift, a bright orange riding jacket, and hopped on my new, oversized, untrained, and equally reluctant bay quarter horse. It was a challenge neither of us was suited for.

It wasn't long before Sergeant started acting up, spooked by the wind creeping up from all sides in his unfamiliar environment. Our half-completed riding ring at Clarity Farm was cold and unforgiving, lacking the layer of soft sand that would have cushioned our dressage practice. It was frozen, uncomfortable, scary, and all wrong.

After many spooks, I decided to quit and try again another day. I met my trainer in the middle of the ring, admitted my defeat, and started to remove my feet from the stirrups to dismount. Sergeant sensed my surrender and took it as his opportunity to bolt for the far-left corner, leaving me suspended in mid-air.

I've always been taught to be tough-minded, so I mistakenly thought as I hung there, *This is going to hurt, but I'll shake it off.* The landing on my tailbone was hard and painful. The impact reverberated up my spine, knocking the wind out of me and leaving me in excruciating pain. My top and bottom halves felt disconnected. When I finally caught my breath, all I could say was "Don't touch me. Please call an ambulance."

As my trainer ran down the hill toward the house and a phone, I lay there as still as possible, clenching every muscle in my core, shivering from pain and cold, alone in the ring on our remote farm. I cried out in pain, searching for comfort and reassurance, but no one was there to hear me at the glorious home on the hill. Clarity Farm was supposed to be a vessel of peace for my family and me. But like the lesson that day, something—everything—was wrong.

After several days in the ICU and surgery by a skilled and empathetic neurosurgeon and her team who inserted a cage in place of my shattered L-2 vertebra, I was recovering. An apparatus helped me breathe. My tailbone and torso were on fire from bruises and nerve damage, and the nerves to my legs were crushed so badly that paralysis was a real concern.

My friends overheard the hospital staff discussing with the cage company sales rep that over 90 percent of people with my injury never walk again. As I was discharged, my neurosurgeon (my hero) confirmed how lucky I was and laid a hand on my still numb leg. She said, "I don't know why you are going to be able to walk again, but you must have an angel on your shoulder."

That is when it all started—the thoughts of *Why me? Why was I spared? What was I put here to do? Am I living my best life, or is there more? I can't waste this blessing, this opportunity to truly LIVE!*

Chapter 3

CLARITY SILENCED

Fast forward a few months, and I found myself stuck at home, recovering with a walker and no neighbors nearby. I relied on the help of my generous friends who fed and carted my kids around. With newfound free time while the kids were at school, I started writing again. I enjoyed writing when I was younger and was told I was an excellent writer, but I had abandoned it (and myself) somewhere along the way.

During that time, *The Oprah Winfrey Show* hosted an essay contest in conjunction with the film release of the book *Divine Secrets of the Ya-Ya Sisterhood*. The essay topic was about how friends have supported you during tough times. Compelled and inspired, I sat in my front office at the Clarity farmhouse that overlooked the gorgeous Little River Valley and wrote and rewrote a humorous yet heartfelt essay.

Once I felt it had the right tone, I submitted it, and it disappeared into the digital ether. Because it had to be typed directly into the website's submission form, I never again saw what I wrote. Imagine my surprise and delight shortly after when I got a phone call from the producer of the *Oprah* show, who said I had won.

But the story doesn't end there. You might be thinking, "Oh wow! How awesome! This is where she discovers herself as a writer and her life changes. She finally finds validation through her gifts, and this story ends happily ever after."

Not so fast.

When the producer asked if the show could film my friends and me on my farm, I declined. (Insert record scratch . . . *who would do that?*)

Oprah was my hero. At the time, I watched her religiously. And yet I was so uncomfortable, misaligned, and insecure in my own home that I wouldn't let the film crew in. It also did not help that *Divine Secrets of the Ya-Ya Sisterhood* featured an unhappy woman trapped in her own beautiful home, a fact I discovered only after winning the contest and starting to read it. *What did I actually write in that disappearing essay anyway?*

Even though I turned down the opportunity to film with the *Oprah* crew, the gracious producer still invited my friends and me to the taping in Chicago. I had many friends from church, the kids' school, and work who helped me, but I could invite only six friends. So I chose the local girls I had been closest to for the longest. They were the ones who had stayed at the hospital while I was in ICU and were the focus of my essay.

I remember one hilarious line in my Oprah *Ya-Ya* essay about one of the gals who burst into my recovery room at the hospital wearing a fuzzy, sophisticated black hat. With the light behind her as she opened the door, it took me a moment in my stupor to realize who it was. I wrote, "I thought it was either the Cat in the Hat or the Grim Reaper entering my room." Something about long-time friends brings a bit of humor into even the worst scenarios and helps you get through them.

Those friends and I flew together to Chicago, accidentally wearing coordinating Ann Taylor outfits. The trend that year was lavender silk. We planned to meet at *The Oprah Winfrey Show* studios before the live taping for a private preview of the movie adaptation of *Divine Secrets of the Ya-Ya Sisterhood*.

After a private viewing of the film, we were bused back to the studio and seated in the second row behind the winners. They were a lovely group of ladies who were supporting their friend—a breast cancer survivor. She was now the focus of the show's primary taped interview since I had refused the film crew's visit to my home. Just feet away from us on the stage with Oprah were the talented and famous actresses from the movie: Sandra Bullock, Ashley Judd, and Ellen Burstyn.

As conciliatory *Ya-Ya* recognition, photos I submitted of our friend group with some of the "petite Ya-Yas" were included in a photo collage at the episode's end. I didn't dare tell my friends that *we* should have been interviewed at my home and seated in the front row. Fear of being discovered kept me silent and unseen for many years after.

For many reasons, which I'll talk more about in the coming chapters, our family eventually moved from Clarity Farm and lived in two "compromise" homes. Ultimately, despite the compromises, no one was satisfied. And so the marriage and the home dissolved. The intentions of living the dream were there, but whose dream was it really? We couldn't happily reach a compromise, so that was the end of it.

Chapter 4
FOR CLARITY'S SAKE

After my divorce, I worked as a corporate controller to make ends meet and support my kids through college. In 2016, I learned that the magnificent home on the hill, Clarity Farm, was going to be torn down. At first I was beside myself. *Why would anyone want to tear down such a beautiful home?*

Even though it was a dream that didn't come true for me, I knew the family who bought Clarity Farm after my horseback riding accident. They thrived there. The community loved the home's unique character and stateliness. When word of the teardown spread, people reached out to me with many fond memories of Clarity Farm.

It got me thinking . . . *homes provide happiness.* They have personalities just like their owners. Even though that home and lifestyle weren't right for me, they brought joy to another family. Now these new owners were going to build something that fit them perfectly on that beautiful piece of property. They were going to create their own Wheel House.

As the Clarity Farm home was torn down to make way for a lovely new showcase home, fate would have it that I was also planning to leave behind my long-held, undesirable job as controller-accountant in the residential construction and design industry. I was drawn to a new path that aligned more closely with my skills and passions: becoming a real estate agent. That role would use my innate talents to create new homes for people.

The timing was perfect. The new showcase tour was set to benefit a charity that supported children with physical disabilities, a cause I genuinely admire and support. That property I found and developed years ago remained stunning, a testament to my "good real estate eye."

I set a goal to become a real estate agent by the time the home was finished. It took me a year to complete the final transformation into who I was meant to be. I wasn't done yet. My beautiful creation, Clarity Farm, might be gone, but I could create new beautiful homes for myself and others—homes that transform, align, and magnify comfort and joy. They would be homes that provided meaning and even served a purpose higher than just a living environment.

By the time the new Clarity Farm showcase home debuted the following year, I had completed the required courses, passed the exam, and obtained my Realtor's license. I resigned from my job as a controller in the design industry and launched my new career as a real estate agent, sponsoring none other than the new Clarity Farm.

Like a phoenix, I recreated myself just as Clarity Farm had—more aligned, purposeful, and authentic than ever. A funny sidenote is that I only told one volunteer at the new Clarity Farm showcase that I had initially developed the property. She graciously kept my secret and was kindly supportive as I walked the grounds and through the house before the showcase tour officially started.

When it came time to publicly unveil the home and give tours to the hordes of visitors, none of the volunteers wanted to do it. So there I was, showing people through the beautiful new home built on the same spot I had built my dream home almost twenty years before, pointing out all the fantastic design features. And all the while I was raising money for the mobility issue charity where I had recovered from my broken back. Talk about déjà vu!

Now, over two decades and eight moves after breaking my back at Clarity Farm, I have reinvented myself and created a new life. I am no longer unseen, misaligned, and living inauthentically.

During this transformative journey, I developed and refined the Wheel House Method to create the best living environment and lifestyle, and become the highest version of myself. I transformed from someone who hid her true self and lived as a false persona to someone who now lives in alignment with her true self, striving to be authentic and live fully in every area of life and home. My mission is to help others discover their true selves and create a lifestyle and home that align with their authenticity, mission, and maximized potential.

Part 2

A HOME FOR YOUR SOUL

Fundamental Theories of the Wheel House Process

Chapter 5

MY TRUE SELF: HOME TRANSFORMATION

Wherever you go, there you are.

—JON KABAT-ZINN

Have you ever heard of the Myers-Briggs Type Indicator (MBTI)? For those unfamiliar with it, a Myers-Briggs ENFP score represents an individual who is Extraverted, iNtuitive, Feeling, and Perceptive—which happens to be where I fall (more on this test in Chapter 7).

Beginning in 2016, I worked with ENFP Life-by-Design coach Dan Johnston, and through that experience, I transitioned from being a small-business controller to a real estate agent. Dan verified my aptitude and skill set for the real estate industry and helped me create a job aligned with my true personality.

The ENFP personality type is known for being high-energy, right-brained, and creative, which makes it less suited for accounting work that requires eight hours a day. As Dan and I worked together to formulate a plan to uplevel and align my life, I repeatedly completed a Wheel of Life analysis, which we'll look at in detail in Chapter 9.

I rated eight areas of my life from 1 to 10 based on my current levels of satisfaction in the categories of Career, Finance, Spirituality, Friends and Family, Environment, Fun and Leisure, Health, and Romance. Each area was affected differently through each of my moves and lifestyle changes.

As my life changed and I came into alignment with my true self, my home life improved. I felt increasingly comfortable and at peace in my home as I transformed into the real me in the present moment.

As I help real estate clients assess their homes and lifestyles, I mentally place each search criterion they mention into one or more of the eight categories of the

Wheel of Life. I compile lists of problems and what it would take for my clients to fix them.

For example, a clear-cut problem in the Career area would be living in a different city than a client's new job. On the Wheel of Life scale for Career, I would rate residing in another town a zero—the current house would not work for the client's work commute.

A less clear issue might be that an open floor plan can create a noisy environment that is less conducive to focusing while working from home. I might rate that as a 7 out of 10 on the scale.

Combining all elements in the eight areas of the Wheel of Life provides a snapshot of what the perfect home could look like for my clients. I also noticed that for both my clients and myself, fixing one area in the Wheel of Life might disrupt another. Thus, all areas must be assessed to minimize the unwanted and unforeseen effects of change on their desired lifestyle.

Finally, I realized that sometimes it isn't even about the house itself. Foundational issues can create strife regardless of location. A misaligned home can stem from invalidation in the 4Ms: Myself, Mastery, Mission, and Mate(s), which we'll dive deeper into in Part 3 of this book.

Just as a structural issue in a house's basement can lead to cracks in the upper floors, misalignment in any of the 4Ms can cause serious lifestyle issues for an individual who is invalidated or disingenuous. Aligning with a false self or persona instead of your true self or soul can cause discomfort, whether conscious or unconscious. Aligning your soul with your home is like having a strong, secure basement or foundation. As magnificent as your home is, if it is misaligned with your true self, it will feel off.

These personal discoveries set me on the path to investigating even deeper aspects of self-discovery and home alignment. As I began to help others find their homes, I realized that sometimes it's not just about the home but also about personal authenticity and living in alignment.

Along with my personal misalignment, studies have shown that happiness, particularly at home, is waning for many Americans. A national report from The Common Good in November 2025 reveals a startling reality: "U.S. happiness is falling at one of the fastest rates in the developed world. . . . The U.S. has fallen from 11th to 24th place in global happiness rankings from 2012 to 2025. . . . while those under 30 rank 62nd globally, reporting declining life satisfaction, purpose, and social support."[1]

This realization has become the basis for not only improving my personal journey toward fulfillment and joy but also the basis for developing the Wheel House Method, especially for our young people as they enter adulthood and make lifestyle decisions that will either improve their happiness or lead to decline.

Chapter 6

THE STATE OF HAPPINESS AT HOME

A home is more than a house. It's a history, a legacy, and a sanctuary of the heart.

—JAMES PATTERSON

After researching recent studies on what people want from their homes and how that connection is falling short, I had a number of interesting discoveries. Let's look at what the numbers say about satisfaction levels with recent homebuyers.

A recent survey by Clever found that about 82 percent of Americans who purchased a home in 2023 or 2024 have at least one regret. Specifically, 24 percent said the home does not meet all their needs, 22 percent felt they bought too quickly, and 12 percent admitted they didn't even like their home.[2]

Approximately 7.8 percent of the US population, or 25 million people, move each year, leaving 12 million dissatisfied with at least one aspect of their home and a whopping 6 million living in a home they dislike—and that's just from those two years of homebuying data.

A follow-up study in May 2025 by the Clever Real Estate Home Buyer Survey found that Americans who bought a home in 2023, 2024, and the beginning of 2025 said they would have made the following changes:

- 20 percent would be more patient if they had a second chance (the most common answer)
- 16 percent would ask more questions
- 14 percent would buy a different home
- 11 percent would take more time to research[3]

The America at Home Study echoed this mindset shift by revealing specific changes in how people live in their homes following the COVID-19 pandemic. Solely focusing on home and community, the results provide comprehensive insight into the impact of wellness on home design and homebuyer satisfaction.

The August 2025 four-wave study highlighted affordability concerns, changing household demographics, and an increasing demand for wellness-supportive environments. Beyond financial wellness concerns, mental, emotional, physical, and environmental issues are now the number-one driver of housing decisions.

Another main finding was the perception of home as safety, now more than ever. From April 2020 to May 2025, most respondents reported feeling less well. When asked in October 2020, "What does home mean to you?" they answered as follows:

- A safe place: 89 percent
- Family: 84 percent
- Freedom: 71 percent
- Financial Stability: 63 percent[4]

These numbers reveal a dramatic shift in financial considerations, household compositions, and consumer values. Still, the August 2025 America at Home Study press release shows the home building and design industry clinging to outdated assumptions about for whom we are building and why. The study highlights the need to realign housing with the contemporary American lifestyle, increasingly shaped by hybrid work, rising wellness expectations, and the urgent demand for more attainable, flexible, and supportive living environments.

Chapter 7

THE HOME AS A REPRESENTATION OF SELF

The ache for home lives in all of us. The safe place where we can go as we are and not be questioned.

—MAYA ANGELOU

I noticed something while changing my life and living environment and then helping hundreds of others as a real estate agent. The state of our home fascinatingly reflects the state of our inner comfort and authenticity. That observation and my previous studies in human resource development led me to a fascination with and research into theories that link the state of our conscious (or unconscious) happiness and development to the soul of our home.

Clare Cooper Marcus's writings prominently highlight the effects of people's intimate relationships with their homes on healing and wellness. *House as a Mirror of Self: Exploring the Deeper Meaning of Home,* published in May 2006, is a profound explanation of how our homes reflect our inner selves and shape our self-image, relationships, and personal growth. Marcus presents a groundbreaking theory of what our relationship to our home says about ourselves, taking readers on a journey from viewing the "house as ego" to seeing the home as a reflection of our souls.

With over twenty-five years of research and case studies, Marcus provides a clear understanding of why you might be feeling uncomfortable in your home. She emphasizes that feeling "at home" is as much about living authentically as it is about choosing the right home.

Marcus further states that the psychological connection individuals and couples have with their homes reminds us that home is more than a location, structure, or aesthetic. Our home choices reflect who we are, and each element of our home affects our mood, relationships, and life. The layout, location, decor, environment, and other aspects of the home create either comfort or discomfort. And each occupant of the home may experience these elements differently.

In *Memories, Dreams, Reflections*, Swiss psychologist Carl Jung equates building a house to assembling our inner self. He describes the gradual evolution of his home on Lake Zurich that he spent over thirty years building. Along the way he added on various towers and annexes to represent his psyche.[5]

Jung believed that the home we dream of can reflect who we are or aspire to be at any given time. He suggested that dreams and the unconscious mind affect and reflect each individual and society.

In *Psychological Types*, Jung laid the groundwork for the MBTI by introducing the study of personality traits such as introversion and extroversion, thinking versus feeling, and sensing versus intuition. In his book, each personality type corresponds to the different ways individuals interact with and contemplate the world around them.[6]

Taking the concept of home as a representation of self even further, I began matching a homeowner's personality type to the type of home and its characteristics to enhance comfort and help them achieve their maximum potential. That was my next logical deduction to help someone live in their Wheel House.

The Myers-Briggs Personality Assessment, developed by mother-daughter duo Katherine Cook Briggs and Isabel Briggs Myers, was designed to help people better understand themselves and others. It categorizes personalities into one of sixteen types based on Carl Jung's initial research.[7]

Based on four pairs of opposite personality traits—Extroverted (E) versus Introverted (I), iNtuitive (N) versus Sensing (S), Feeling (F) versus Thinking (T), and Judging (J) versus Perceiving (P)—the questions establish a four-letter personality preference using one dominant letter from each category. A four-letter acronym such as ISFJ represents one of the sixteen personality types, each with its own set of characteristics for how a person functions internally and externally.

Understanding your MBTI can reveal not only how you best operate in the world but also what type of home environment suits your personality's preferences. For example, an introverted personality might like a home with quiet spaces for contemplation, while an extrovert might enjoy space for entertaining.

An intuitive-feeler might operate more often on the right (creative) side of the brain, requiring a space that encourages their artistic or people-focused endeavors. In contrast, a sensing-thinker might need space to work on concrete, absolute (left-brained) ideas. Each MBTI type would naturally have different preferences for the characteristics of living spaces that best exemplify and support their personalities.

Let's look at a more complete example of two opposites on the MBTI: an ISTJ (Introverted, Sensing, Thinking, Judging) type and an ENFP (Extroverted, iNtuitive, Feeling, Perceiving) type. For the ISTJ, imagine a private space, if not an entirely private home, dedicated to contemplation and planning. This space might be full of notes, to-do lists, a calendar to keep on task, closet systems for organization, home filing systems, and everything in its proper place.

On the other hand, for the ENFP, envision a messy workspace full of inspiration for free thinking, or even a free-flowing creative space. They may prefer being close to a community that offers inspiration and diversion from anything they find routine or monotonous. They would appreciate rooms or outdoor space for entertaining.

The Odd Couple TV show from the 1970s illustrates these two contrasting personality types living together. Felix, a neat and uptight professional photographer, seemed to be an ISFJ; Oscar, the cigar-smoking, free-spirited writer (fun-loving slob), showed ENTP tendencies. Both drove each other nuts but also balanced each other out by providing insights and support. The characters frequently disagreed over maintaining their living space and their contrasting approaches to life. The humorous clash between Felix's need for order, health consciousness, and cleanliness, and Oscar's chaotic, carefree, and messy lifestyle made for an entertaining and award-winning show.

Consider yourself and your loved ones living at home with your personality types and lifestyle preferences. Do you clash in certain areas? Do you complement each other and fill in any voids when running a household? Could any disagreements stem from how you were made rather than disrespect, simply reflecting differing living preferences? When reading through the Wheel House Assessment, consider your own innate preferences as they relate to your personality. If possible, incorporate everyone's personality preferences when seeking a compromise on the Wheel House as a couple or family.

There are many free MBTI tests online if you are curious. Many other personality type tests such as the Enneagram, DISC, and Big Five Inventory provide insight into your innate personality characteristics. I have included only the MBTI here for simplicity as it focuses on observable behaviors and cognitive functions to explain how you process information and interact with the world. The Myers-Briggs provides insights into how you perceive the world and make decisions, which is helpful for understanding how people process information, communicate, and collaborate.

We'll discuss personality more in Chapter 11 where we define your true self.

MTBI Personality Types Key

 EXTROVERTS are energized by people, enjoy a variety of tasks, a quick pace and are good at multitasking.

 INTROVERTS often like working alone or in small groups, prefer a more deliberate pace, and like to focus on one task at a time

 THINKERS tend to make decisions using logical analysis, objectively weigh pros and cons, and value honesty, consistency and fairness

 FEELERS tend to be sensitive and cooperative, and decide based on their own personal values and how others will be affected by their actions.

 SENSORS are realistic people who like to focus on the facts and details, and apply common sense and past experience to come up with practical solutions.

 INTUITIVES are energized by people, enjoy a variety of tasks, a quick pace and are good at multitasking.

 JUDGERS tend to be organized and prepared, like to make and stick to plans, and are comfortable following most rules.

 PERCEIVERS prefer to keep their options open, like to be able to act spontaneously and like to be flexible with making plans.

The three home-as-a-representation-of-self theories form the basis for the first steps of the Wheel House Method. Identifying characteristics of your true self or soul is the first step to creating an environment of alignment and support, and thus comfort and joy. Next, we will explore the other theories that underpin the Wheel House Method.

Chapter 8

MASLOW'S HIERARCHY IN YOUR HOME

Let's dive into Maslow's hierarchy and how it applies to your home. Abraham Maslow introduced the concept of a hierarchy of needs in 1943 in a paper titled "A Theory of Human Motivation"[8] and later in a book, *Motivation and Personality*.[9] In this hierarchy, Maslow suggests that people are motivated to fulfill basic needs at the bottom of the pyramid before moving up to other, more advanced needs.

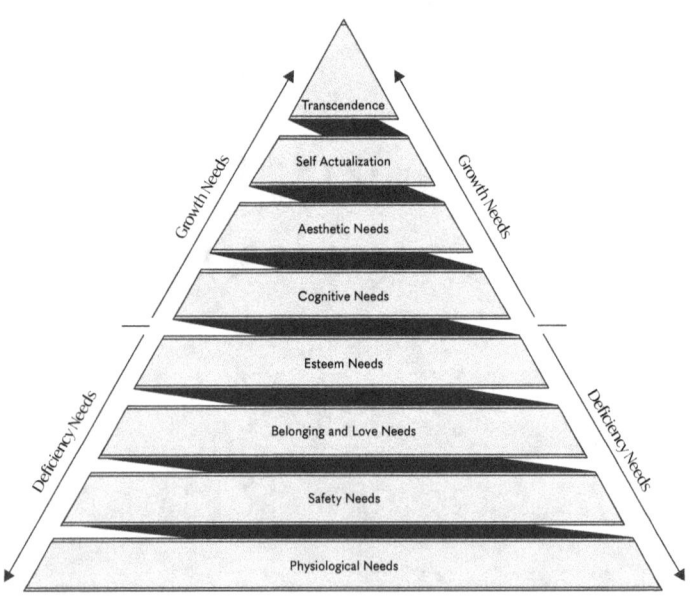

Maslow's hierarchy provides a scale of increasing satisfaction, ranging from basic needs such as water and shelter to self-actualization and transcendence. Living authentically, transcending, and helping others are said to be among the ultimate measures of success and happiness. While there is some evidence of reaching higher needs on Maslow's scale without first meeting some of the fundamental needs (e.g., a person without shelter still feeling the love and belonging of their family), the general flow is toward the pyramid's apex, from physiological needs to transcendence.

Physiological, safety, belonging, love, and esteem needs are felt as deficiencies. In contrast, cognitive, aesthetic, self-actualization, and transcendent needs are associated with personal growth. The turning point from addressing deficiencies to pursuing growth and potential fulfillment lies between esteem and cognitive needs. Logically, experiencing a deficiency need would weigh more heavily on the need to align your home environment than a higher growth need.

In ascending order, here is a brief description of Maslow's needs categories as they apply to the home. At the lowest level are physiological needs. In your living situation, that might mean access to clean water, a roof over your head to protect you from the elements, warmth in the cold, accessible food, and a place to store clothes and sleep.

Without meeting those needs, our bodies struggle to maintain physical homeostasis. In Maslow's theory, we address the lowest concerns before moving on to higher needs. For example, if you are hungry, cold, or thirsty, you would address these basic needs before considering where you might feel you fit in (love and belonging) or picking the perfect wallpaper for your powder room (aesthetic).

I am grateful that my clients have met these physiological needs. However, I realize that this is not the case for many people worldwide. I am drawn to helping those who are struggling to meet their most basic needs and freedoms in their homes and communities. Please don't miss the Afterword of this book where I talk about some of my favorite charities that offer housing as a first step to those struggling to live fully and authentically. I will be donating a portion of the profits from this book to charities that support recovery and veterans' housing programs.

Safety needs—the next level up—might involve living in a safe neighborhood, having adequate fire and police protection, and being free from water intrusion, radon gas, mold, and harm from others. Those needs also include homeownership issues such as affording homeowner's insurance or saving for emergencies after basic living expenses.

According to Maslow, the next need is to feel loved and accepted by family, friends, and possibly a romantic partner. Feeling loved and being part of a group positively impact both physical and mental health. Making space in your home to encourage love and belonging might look like a large kitchen for family gatherings or a primary bedroom with adequate closet space and bedside table arrangements to attract the love of your life. You might also consider how the neighborhood and town contribute to feelings of belonging.

Esteem needs form the next level of the hierarchy and refer to feeling good about yourself and being valued by others. Self-confidence and having your contributions appreciated can eliminate feelings of inferiority. That might mean having avenues in your community and home that promote your skills and interests and, in the best-case scenario, a home that reflects your true self and desired station in life.

Cognitive needs come next on the hierarchy. They involve the desire for meaning and motivation to acquire knowledge and education. Curiosity and comprehension fuel the need to learn. In your home, that might look like a library or shelves full of books on your favorite subjects or by your favorite authors. It may also mean taking courses at your local university or county extension. Creating space in the home for self-development and pursuing interests is a higher-level need in Maslow's hierarchy of needs, which leads to self-actualization.

After meeting cognitive needs, individuals progress to aesthetic needs to enhance the beauty of their lives. Surrounding yourself with beauty and comfort is the last step toward achieving self-actualization. That might look like having a lovely walking trail or art galleries nearby. Inside your home, you might have a pottery studio, a display of favorite travel finds, or a color scheme that complements your style and self-expression. By discovering your style choices, expressing them in your home, and connecting with nature and beauty in your environment, you cultivate and express an intimacy with yourself and the world around you.

Maslow describes reaching your full potential, or self-actualization, as the desire to accomplish everything possible and become the most you can be. Whether it's becoming the best parent, partner, artist, athlete, entrepreneur, clergy member, or inventor, fulfilling the ascending needs makes aspirations more attainable. Think of Maslow's hierarchy as a stepping-up process that eliminates lower-level barriers to achieve higher-level goals. In your home, that involves evaluating your current home environment and creating a lifestyle that eliminates obstacles and supports values and goals.

According to Maslow, there's a step beyond self-actualization that represents the ultimate achievement in your lifetime: transcendence. Maslow explains transcendence as "the very highest and most inclusive and holistic levels of human consciousness, behaving and relating, as ends rather than means, to oneself, to significant others, to human beings in general, to other species, to nature, and to the cosmos."[10] In giving the fullest of yourself to something beyond personal interests, you root deeply in your current society while approaching diverse perspectives and contributing to the common good. Regardless of your religious or spiritual beliefs, you can reach the highest plane of existence through transcendence, using your gifts to serve humanity and the universe, thereby raising the collective consciousness.

This book aims to apply Maslow's hierarchy of needs assessment to each of the eight areas of the Wheel of Life in order to help you evaluate your current living situation, identify barriers, and create an ideal environment to support your path to self-actualization.

Chapter 9
THE WHEEL OF LIFE

Paul J. Meyer, founder of the Success Motivation Institute in 1960, conceived the popular coaching tool, the Wheel of Life. Meyer was a coaching industry pioneer focused on programs that empower people to achieve their goals. His Wheel of Life concept continues to help individuals set goals, create action plans, and improve their lives by examining the eight life areas.[11]

Wheel House Assessment

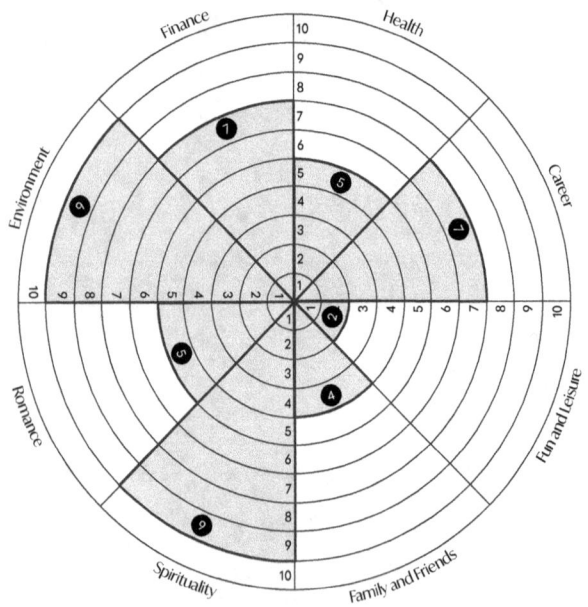

In life coaching, the Wheel of Life categories balance the client's life and prioritize different life goals. You can review and assess these changing life goals quarterly, annually, or during a significant life change such as marriage, divorce, the birth of a child, the death of a partner, a job promotion, a career shift, or retirement.

In my many years as a top-performing real estate agent, I have observed that life changes often necessitate home changes. The Wheel House Assessment uses the Wheel of Life to examine how your current living situation compares with your ideal lifestyle across eight areas: Health, Career, Fun and Leisure, Family and Friends, Spirituality, Romance, Environment, and Finance.

Chapter 10

THE WHEEL HOUSE METHOD: A COMPLETE PROCESS

Here are some typical definitions of the word *wheelhouse*:

1. Your area of interest, skills, or expertise
2. As a baseball term, a pitch within the zone that is most advantageous for a batter to hit a home run
3. A place or center of control or leadership within an organization
4. A nautical pilothouse, a protected area from where the captain steers the vessel
5. *Wheel House*: A home with the foundational elements of My Self, Master, Mission, and Mate(s) that supports the lifestyle elements of Career, Finance, Environment, Health, Career, Fun and Leisure, Family and Friends, Spirituality, Romance, Environment, and Finance, and aligns with and expresses the genuine individuality of its owner(s).

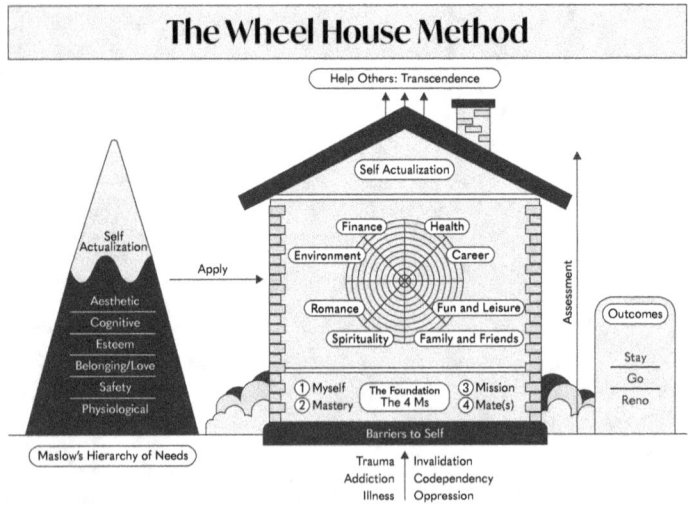

Real estate has long operated under a simple premise: Tell me your budget and your square footage needs, and I'll find you a house. But what if those criteria are the wrong place to start?

The Wheel House Method flips the script entirely. Instead of beginning with properties, we start with *you*. It's not the version of you that fits neatly into market data or mortgage calculators; it's the whole, authentic you—the person navigating career transitions and relationship dynamics, the person balancing health needs with financial realities, the person trying to create a home that supports the life you're living right now.

This chapter lays out the complete framework—a visual and conceptual journey that shows how your home can become a vessel for holistic well-being and self-actualization. Whether you decide to stay in your current space, search for something new, or renovate what you have, this process ensures that your decision is rooted in clarity rather than crisis.

The Foundation: The 4Ms

Every journey toward an aligned life must begin on solid ground. The Foundation layer consists of what I call the 4Ms—four fundamental pillars that anchor your existence and inform every choice you make about where and how you live.

My Self grounds everything in your individual identity and personal well-being. This is about honoring who you are at your core—your personality, your values, and your life goals. It's the foundation's foundation, if you will.

Mastery encompasses your skills, expertise, and professional growth. It's where your career intersects with your competence and contribution. A home that supports mastery might include a functional home office, proximity to professional networks, or space for continuing education and skill development.

Mission is your purpose—what you're called to contribute to the world. It is the *why* beneath your daily actions. Whether you're raising children, building a nonprofit, creating art, providing jobs for many, or serving your community, your mission needs a home that can hold it.

Mate(s) represents your primary relationships and partnership. This isn't just about romantic relationships; it's about the person or people with whom you're building a life. Are you single and fiercely independent? Partnered with aligned visions? Co-parenting across two households? Your Mate(s) status fundamentally shapes what home needs to provide.

The Wheel of Life: Eight Essential Areas

Once we've established your foundation, we move to the heart of the assessment: the Wheel of Life. This framework, adapted from life-coaching practices and reimagined through a real estate lens, examines eight essential life areas your home directly impacts. We will examine the following areas in depth in later chapters.

Health examines how your physical environment supports or sabotages your well-being. Can you move your body easily? Is there natural light? Does the space promote restful sleep? Does the kitchen inspire nourishing meals?

Career looks at how your living situation supports your professional life. Can you work from home effectively? Is your commute sustainable? Are you in a location that connects you to opportunity?

Fun and Leisure addresses your capacity for joy, play, and relaxation. Do you have room to host friends? Space for hobbies? Access to cultural activities? A home that doesn't make room for fun is a home that slowly suffocates the soul.

Family and Friends evaluates the proximity to your support network and your capacity to maintain meaningful relationships. Are you isolated? Well-connected? Able to host the people you love?

Spirituality speaks to your need for meaning, reflection, and connection to something larger than yourself. That could manifest as a meditation space, access to nature, or a corner where you can think, breathe, or pray.

Romance considers whether your space nurtures intimacy and connection in your primary relationship. Do you have privacy? Shared spaces that bring you together? Room to maintain your individual identities?

Environment assesses your relationship with your physical surroundings—the neighborhood, the natural world, and the aesthetic quality of your daily landscape. Does your environment energize you or deplete you?

Finance examines the hard math of affordability and investment. Are you house-poor? Are you building equity? Are you positioned for future financial freedom? That is where dreams meet spreadsheets.

During a Wheel House assessment, we score each of these eight areas on a scale of 1 to 10, with 10 representing complete alignment and satisfaction. The resulting visual—imagine a wheel with eight spokes of varying lengths—reveals exactly where your life is out of balance and how your current living situation might be contributing to that imbalance.

What makes this approach powerful is its honesty. Most people who are moving through the traditional real estate process don't realize their marriage is struggling until they're fighting about kitchen layouts. They don't recognize their isolation until they're signing closing papers on a house forty minutes from their best friend. The Wheel of Life makes the invisible visible before you're contractually committed.

Maslow's Hierarchy in Your Home

Maslow gave us a framework for understanding human needs as a hierarchy—from basic physiological requirements at the bottom to self-actualization at the peak. The Wheel House Method applies this same progression to your living space, recognizing that homes can either support or hinder your journey up this pyramid.

Physiological needs are the baseline. Does your home provide shelter, clean water, functional utilities, and basic safety from the elements? If these aren't met, nothing else matters.

Safety encompasses both physical security and psychological stability. Is your neighborhood safe? Are your locks functional? Do you feel secure in your space? Can you afford your mortgage without constant anxiety?

Belonging and Love emerge once safety is established. Does your home allow you to build and maintain relationships? Can you host gatherings? Are you part of a community? Or are you so isolated that loneliness has become your default state?

Esteem requires space that reflects your accomplishments and allows you to pursue achievement. Can you take pride in your home? Does it support your professional success? Do you have room for the activities that build your confidence?

Cognitive needs involve intellectual stimulation and growth. Is there space for learning, reading, or creative problem-solving? Are you surrounded by inspiration or visual chaos that drains your mental energy?

Aesthetic needs speak to beauty and order. Humans need environments that please the eye and soothe the soul. This isn't superficial; it's essential. An ugly or chaotic space literally impacts your well-being.

Self-actualization is the peak of personal development—becoming your fullest, most authentic self. A home that reaches this level provides space for deep work, creative expression, and the pursuit of your highest potential.

Transcendence sits at the very top—the capacity to move beyond your own needs and contribute meaningfully to others. When your home fully supports your life, you're free to focus outward, to serve, to help, and to give back.

Here's the critical insight: You can't skip levels. If your basic safety needs aren't met, if you're drowning in mortgage debt or living in an unsafe neighborhood, you're not going to experience self-actualization in that space. The traditional real estate approach often sells people homes that meet higher-level needs (granite countertops, spa bathrooms) while ignoring foundational cracks in safety or belonging. The Wheel House Method ensures that you build from the bottom up.

Barriers to Self: What Stands in the Way

Before we can align our homes with our authentic lives, we need to acknowledge what prevents us from accessing that authenticity in the first place. Those barriers aren't personal failings; they're human realities that shape our decision-making, often unconsciously.

Trauma carries unresolved emotional wounds that influence how we see and use space. Someone who grew up in chaos might crave order to an extreme. Someone who experienced violence might struggle with ground-floor bedrooms. Trauma informs our choices whether we recognize it or not.

Addiction—whether to substances, work, shopping, or other dependencies—drains resources and distorts priorities. You can't make clear decisions about where to live when you're not clear-headed about anything.

Illness, both physical and mental, shapes our needs and limitations in profound ways. Chronic pain requires different spaces than chronic anxiety. Depression demands a different light, while mobility issues demand accessibility.

Invalidation—past experiences of being dismissed, unseen, or told your needs don't matter—erodes your confidence in knowing what you want. If you've spent years being told your preferences are wrong, you might not even trust your own assessment of what home should feel like.

Codependency entangles your needs with others to the point where you can't distinguish between *what I want* and *what they need me to want*. That makes authentic home decisions nearly impossible because you're not sure which voice is yours.

Oppression—systemic barriers related to race, class, disability, gender, sexuality, or other marginalized identities—limits choices and opportunities in concrete ways. Not everyone has equal access to safe neighborhoods, fair lending, or welcoming communities.

The Wheel House Method doesn't pretend to solve these barriers. That often requires therapeutic work, community support, or systemic change. But by naming them, we create space to work around them honestly. If you know you're dealing with unresolved trauma, you can approach house-hunting with that awareness rather than being blindsided by your visceral reactions to certain spaces. If you recognize codependent patterns, you can build in accountability to ensure your choices reflect your actual needs.

These barriers sit at the foundation of the Wheel House framework—literally on the ground supporting it—as a reminder that self-knowledge requires honesty about what stands between us and living fully as our true selves.

The Assessment Journey

With the Wheel House Foundation, the Wheel of Life, and Maslow's hierarchy all in view, we begin the actual assessment process. This isn't a quick online quiz or a single conversation; it's a structured exploration that typically unfolds over several sessions.

We start by establishing where you are right now across all eight life areas. Then we map your current living situation in those eight areas against Maslow's hierarchy. Are your basic needs covered? Where are the gaps? Are you stuck trying to achieve self-actualization in a space that doesn't meet your safety needs?

That means asking questions that traditional real estate never touches. How's your marriage actually doing? When was the last time you had friends over? Do you have space for the hobbies that feed your soul? Are you sleeping well? Can you afford this house without constant stress?

Throughout this process, we're watching for misalignments. Maybe your Career spoke is thriving, but your Romance and Friends/Family spokes are lower because your commute eats up every spare hour. Maybe your Finance spoke looks great on paper, but your Health spoke is suffering because you can't afford to leave a home with mold issues. Maybe your Environment spoke scores high, but your Spirituality spoke is nonexistent because you're so far from the church community you care about.

The assessment reveals not just where you are but why, and that why is what empowers you to make a different choice.

Three Outcomes: Stay, Go, or Renovate

After working through the Wheel House Assessment, you arrive at one of three intentional decisions. Notice I said intentional—not impulsive, not reactive, not based on what the market's doing or what your neighbor just decided to do. These outcomes emerge from clarity.

Stay means you've determined that your current home can be transformed to serve your life better. It could be a matter of rearranging furniture, establishing better boundaries around work-from-home space, or simply recognizing that proximity to your support network outweighs the kitchen you wish were bigger. Staying is often the least expensive and least disruptive option, but only if it's a genuine choice rather than a lack of clarity.

Go means it's time to move to a space that aligns with where you are now—not where you were when you bought the place and not where you imagine you might be someday, but who you actually are in this season of life. That might mean downsizing after the kids leave, relocating for a relationship or career opportunity, or finally getting out of the starter home that never quite fit. Going requires courage, logistics, and usually money, but it also offers a clean slate.

Reno means renovating to bridge the gap between your home and your needs. It is the middle path—keeping what works (location, community, memories) while changing what doesn't (layout, functionality, aesthetics). Renovation can be expensive and disruptive, but it allows you to create precisely what you need without losing what you love.

None of these outcomes is inherently better than the others. The right choice depends entirely on your specific situation, your Wheel House Assessment, and your position on Maslow's hierarchy. What matters is that whichever path you choose, it's rooted in self-knowledge rather than panic or pressure.

Help Others, Ego, and Transcendence

At the peak of the Wheel House journey sits what I call Self Actualization—the ultimate expression of living in alignment. That level acknowledges three interconnected elements.

Help Others represents the capacity to contribute meaningfully beyond your own needs. When your home fully supports your life—when your basic needs are covered, your relationships are thriving, your health is prioritized, your purpose is clear—you're free to focus outward. You have energy to volunteer, mentor, create, or serve. Your home becomes a launching pad for impact rather than a constant drain on your resources.

Ego isn't a dirty word in this framework. It represents healthy self-regard, the pride that comes from living authentically, and the satisfaction of creating a home that reflects who you truly are. There's nothing wrong with wanting your space to feel like an achievement as long as that achievement is measured by your own values rather than keeping up with someone else's highlight reel.

Transcendence is the highest human capacity—the ability to move beyond self-actualization into connection with something larger than yourself. In the context of home, that might mean creating a space that serves as a gathering place for community, a sanctuary for healing, or a workshop for meaningful work that ripples outward.

This peak isn't some fantasy reserved for the wealthy or the enlightened. It's available to anyone willing to do the work of alignment. I've seen it in modest homes where every corner serves a purpose and every choice reflects the owner's values. I've seen it absent in mansions where residents are drowning in maintenance, debt, and disconnection from what actually matters to them.

The difference isn't money; it's intentionality.

Why This Process Works

The Wheel House Method works because it reverses the traditional real estate equation. Instead of asking what you can afford and then trying to make your life fit that box, it asks, *Who are you?* and then finds the space that fits your life.

This isn't slower; it's actually faster because you're not wasting time looking at properties that will never serve you. It's not more expensive; it often saves people from costly mistakes motivated by panic or social pressure. And it's not indulgent; it's practical because a home that doesn't support your actual life is one you'll either outgrow quickly or slowly suffocate in.

The framework also creates accountability. When you've scored your eight life areas and identified the gaps, you can't unsee that information. When you've acknowledged the barriers standing between you and authentic choice, you're forced to reckon with them. When you've mapped your Wheel of Life needs against Maslow's hierarchy, you know exactly which level needs attention first.

Most importantly, the process honors the full complexity of being human. It doesn't reduce you to a credit score and a wish list. It doesn't pretend that homes are just buildings rather than containers for our entire lives. It treats your housing decision as what it actually is: one of the most significant choices you'll make, worthy of depth, reflection, and care.

Moving Forward

Understanding the Wheel House framework is one thing; actually applying it to your own life is another. The chapters that follow will take you deeper into each component, exploring the 4Ms in detail, breaking down each spoke of the Wheel of Life, and walking through real-life case studies of people who have used this process to make transformative decisions about where and how they live.

But before we dive into those specifics, please sit with this overview. Look at the visual map. The Wheel House Method as a whole is illustrated by the whole house from the ground and foundation, through the living areas, and up to the attic. The Wheel House Assessment focuses on the main floor, your actual living environment where you examine the eight areas of the Wheel of Life. Notice where your attention is drawn. What speaks to you? What makes you uncomfortable? What excites you?

Be aware that your home already knows things about you that you might not have admitted to yourself yet. It knows where you're out of balance. It knows which needs are being met and which are being ignored. It knows whether you're building toward self-actualization or stuck maintaining a facade that's exhausting you.

The Wheel House Method simply gives you the language and structure to hear what your home is trying to tell you and, more importantly, to respond with intention.

Welcome to the journey. Let's figure out where you actually belong.

Part 3

THE WHEEL HOUSE FOUNDATION

The 4Ms

Chapter 11

MY SELF

Be yourself. Everyone else is already taken.

—OSCAR WILDE

I gathered the various definitions of *self* from the dictionary and other disciplines in the sciences, and then added the definition from the perspective of the Wheel House Method as follows:

1. Your basic personality or nature, especially considered in terms of what you are really like as a person. Personality, character, temperament, identity.
2. A person's essential being that distinguishes them from others, especially considered as the object of introspection or reflexive action.
3. The totality of the individual that encompasses all characteristic attributes, both conscious and unconscious, mental and physical.
4. The essential qualities that make one person distinct from all others. The unified being that is the source of consciousness.
5. A relatively stable set of perceptions of who people are in relation to themselves, others, and social systems.
6. A process that orchestrates an individual's personal experience, after which they become self-aware and self-reflective about their place in society.
7. *Wheel House.* The first step for alignment: living from the essence of your being, authentic self, or soul. In alignment with who you were made and meant to be.

Understanding yourself is the true north of this process. Being several degrees off course can leave you in a misaligned living space.

The first step in creating your ultimate lifestyle is to recognize your true nature—your gifts, personality, and values. We are born with certain personality traits and temperaments. But over the years, many of us often morph into a person others want us to be, giving up parts of ourselves because of trauma, influence, or fear.

After living much of my life under these circumstances, I, like many people, reached a point where I no longer recognized myself. I was lost. I felt scared, alone, and unrecognizable from the self-assured, athletic, intelligent, creative, and empathetic person I was born to be. I had let others tell me that I was too much—too much personality, too strong, too optimistic, too creatively bold to fit into the stoic and linear world into which I was born. The goals that were set for me were not my own. I succumbed to peer pressure, bigotry, the status quo, limited thinking, and a world that seems to value data and money over personality and living freely.

Uncovering your true self involves identifying your core attributes—personality, values, desires, skills, and interests. This true self is separate from the false self, the modified persona developed to gain approval or survive earlier in life. It is genuine and unaffected by external factors.

According to renowned psychologists, finding your true self involves consciously creating a lifestyle aligned with your individual goals and desires. Psychologist Carl Rogers believed personal choices were more constrained in the past, and the freedom and autonomy in most modern societies enable authentic living and greater mental, spiritual, and human well-being.[12] English psychoanalyst

Donald Winnicott described the true self as a sense of self based on spontaneous, authentic experiences, embodying a real self with little to no contradiction.[13]

The journey to self-discovery can include journaling your thoughts, feelings, and experiences; practicing mindfulness techniques such as meditation and conscious observation; and engaging in self-dialogue such as *What mattered to me when I was young?* and *What truly moves me?* These mechanisms can reveal your desires and values.

Understanding the different facets of your personality through tools such as the MBTI and the Enneagram is an additional way to define your true self. The MBTI, based on Carl Jung's theory of psychological types, focuses on observable traits and cognitive preferences—how you perceive the world and process information. On the other hand, the Enneagram, dating back to ancient Greece and popularized by Claudio Naranjo in the 1970s, focuses on the underlying motivations, fears, and desires that drive your behavior. It offers a more holistic, complex perspective on personal growth. You can find free assessments for both the MBTI and Enneagram tests online. By using both systems you can gain a richer, more nuanced understanding of yourself and those around you, constructing an environment where you can thrive.

Chapter 12

MASTERY

The more aware of your intentions and your experiences you become, the more you will be able to create the two, and the more you will be able to create the experiences of your life consciously. This is the development of mastery. It is the creation of authentic power.

—GARY ZUKAV

The following are definitions of *mastery*:

1. Comprehensive knowledge or skill in a subject or accomplishment
2. The act or process of becoming an expert in something
3. Humanistic self-actualization
4. *Wheel House:* The second step in the Wheel House Foundation where you identify gifts and focus on mastering those talents to serve others.

Why is mastery so important? Because it allows us to focus on something bigger than ourselves and our egos. By recognizing our gifts and talents, and applying that knowledge to a field of study, we can help others gain understanding, potentially cure diseases, or enlighten someone to pay it forward.

Wonder is a lovely thing. When others marvel at what an artist, performer, or educator offers to the world, it provides that expert with a sense of pride. Their accomplishments outweigh their insecurities as they bask in the warm feeling of appreciation and being truly recognized for their gifts and contributions to society.

Can you imagine the world without Michelangelo's paintings, Einstein's theory of relativity, Madame Curie's discoveries, Gandhi's nonviolent resistance, Muhammad Ali's heavyweight skills, Beethoven's *Symphony No. 5*, or Mother Teresa's charity work? The world would not be as vibrant and full of beauty, kindness, or progressive thinking.

In your own life, you might think, *Well, that's a tall order*. After all, Michelangelo admitted, "If people knew how hard I worked to get my mastery, it wouldn't seem so wonderful at all." While there is merit to his statement, I'm grateful that he persisted and made his masterpiece on the ceiling of the Sistine Chapel.

You can rest knowing that not all of us are meant to be masters of the arts, brilliant scientists, or world leaders. But we can be the best parents, grade school teachers, builders, bus drivers, doctors, comedians, or local politicians by using our unique mastery to bring light, life, security, and health to others and to our planet.

Marc Rosenburg, contributor to *Learning Solutions* magazine, outlines four stages on the journey to mastery:

- Novice: You are new to the job—an apprentice.
- Competent: You can perform tasks to the basic standards—a journeyman.
- Experienced: You are flexible to different situations and seek to customize knowledge and resources to achieve the best results—the seeker of knowledge.
- Mastery: Through collaboration, research, and problem-solving, you create better or unique solutions—the expert.[14]

James Clear highlights these three benefits of mastery in the creative process:

1. Discovery of Self: Our true thoughts and feelings emerge by channeling our energies into the creative process. Pursuing mastery, we dedicate the time and energy needed to discover our true selves.

2. **Fulfillment:** There are moments when you complete a project or finish work and think, *I was meant to do this. I am headed in the right direction; this is my calling.* The pride that comes with this acknowledgment is a byproduct of continually striving to do your best.
3. **Opportunity for Growth:** New opportunities will arise when people sense your enthusiasm and dedication, and spread the word about your creations and achievements.[15]

I didn't set out to master real estate—I set out to solve a problem I kept seeing. Coming from a background as a controller in residential construction and design, I understood jobs, numbers, and systems. But when I transitioned to real estate, I noticed something the spreadsheets couldn't capture: a fundamental disconnect between how people were living post-pandemic and how the industry was serving them.

People weren't just looking for square footage anymore. They were searching for homes that could hold their new hybrid work lives, their reprioritized relationships, their rediscovered hobbies, and their need for sanctuary. The world had shifted, but the questions we were asking clients hadn't.

That's when the Wheel House Method was born. It asks clients to get honest about who they are and how they actually want to live before we ever talk about granite countertops or school districts. When your home aligns with your authentic life, everything flows differently.

True mastery means learning how to share this framework across different platforms. On American Dream TV, I distill complex lifestyle concepts into moments that resonate on screen. With my *Live in Your Wheel House* podcast and YouTube channel, I weave together voices such as Clare Cooper Marcus and Carl Jung with real-world stories. In this book, I create a lasting resource readers can return to as their lives evolve.

Each medium requires its own skills, yet threading through them is a consistent voice—engaging, empathetic, enthusiastic, insightful, and always in service of helping people live more intentionally. Looking back at my journey from controller to Top 5% real estate agent, I see that mastery isn't about abandoning what you knew before; it's about integrating it into what you're becoming.

My analytical skills didn't disappear; they evolved. Now I analyze human needs, market trends driven by lifestyle shifts, and property potential through the lens of authentic living. I apply the precision of accounting to the art of matching people with spaces that could transform their lives.

Mastery requires vulnerability. Every time I step in front of a camera or hit record on a podcast, I'm putting myself out there. And that's necessary because mastery isn't about being perfect; it's about being willing to grow in public, refine your thinking, and admit when you don't have all the answers.

The Wheel House Method continues to evolve as I work with more clients and deepen my understanding of how homes shape lives. Mastery is less about arriving and more about the commitment to keep showing up, keep learning, and keep serving at the highest level you're capable of today.

Chapter 13

MISSION

Outstanding people have one thing in common: an absolute sense of mission.

—ZIG ZIGLAR

Here are some definitions of *mission*:

1. An important goal or purpose that is accompanied by strong conviction; a calling or vocation
2. Any work that someone believes it is their duty to do
3. Any vital task or duty that is assigned, allotted, or self-imposed
4. *Wheel House*: The third step in identifying and building the supportive foundation of the Wheel House Method. Committing to a mission to help others with innate gifts you have mastered is the third key to creating a solid lifestyle foundation.

When we align our path with our talents, that's where the magic happens. As we grow up, the untamed world often tries to dictate who we should be. Well-intentioned parents, teachers, societal norms, popular culture, naysayers, and people with ulterior motives can steer us away from our God-given gifts.

Even worse, sometimes we feel as though we have no mission or gifts at all. In effect, we mistakenly believe we don't matter. But we all matter. We were all given special gifts that, when used to achieve mastery, make for a fulfilling life and an elevated world. We all have a duty, whether we recognize it or not, to leave this world better than we found it by using our special gifts.

Just as the periodic table in chemistry illustrates the diversity of elements, the world was created with different kinds of people, each possessing inherent talents intended to help our world thrive through the division of labor. People with various skills and aptitudes are spread around the globe. When we discover how we were made, commit to mastering our gifts, and apply them to a personal mission, it benefits both our lives and the lives of others.

Furthermore, much like chemistry, combining our talents with others' complementary ones creates what Gino Wickman and Mark Winters call Rocket Fuel in their book of the same name.[16] This blend of talents is the genius behind innovation and success.

How can you tell what your mission is? If you master your talents and listen to your heart, you'll be unable to resist the opportunities that arise. Your mission will creep into your subconscious and whisper to you, refusing to be ignored. Seemingly serendipitous events will continuously offer signs, teachers, and cohorts.

Your mission will be unique to you. Once you recognize your strengths, you will fulfill your destiny if you are open to the signs that guide you to mastery and a specific mission. Pray, meditate, be still, and let it fill you with an unstoppable desire. Your gifts are uniquely yours, and your job is to master them and apply them to a mission that makes this world better.

According to *Inc.* magazine, identifying your personal mission provides the following benefits:

1. It integrates your identity with a unifying direction.
2. It provides a focus to build on past successes, creating a cohesive theme that amplifies your effort.
3. It simplifies decision-making.
4. It holds you accountable for your decisions and actions.[17]

My mission is to help others discover their true selves and create a lifestyle and home that align with their authenticity, mission, and maximized potential. But here's the thing about mission: It can't just live in your head or on a page; it has to show up in how you actually live.

When I look around my home, I see my mission reflected back at me. My office isn't just a place to work; it's designed to fuel creativity and connection. There's space for recording podcast episodes, a setup for virtual client meetings, and a corner dedicated to writing where natural light pours in. Because my mission involves helping others discover themselves, I need a space that helps me stay connected to my own voice and vision.

My kitchen tells another story. It's not magazine-perfect, but it's set up for the spontaneous gatherings with people like my Sippin' Sistas, the impromptu strategy sessions, and the celebration after a client finds their perfect home. My mission is about authentic connection, so my kitchen prioritizes function and flow over showroom aesthetics. It's where relationships deepen, not where I stress about perfection.

My bedroom is my sanctuary for restoration because I can't help others maximize their potential if I'm running on empty. The space is intentionally calming, free from work clutter, and designed to support the rest I need to show up fully for my clients and community.

Here's what living my mission has taught me: Your home should be the physical manifestation of what matters most to you. If I'm asking clients to align their homes with their authenticity, I have to be willing to do the same. Every room serves my mission: to connect, to create, to serve, and to rest so I can do it all again tomorrow.

Chapter 14

MATE(S)

Lots of people want to ride with you in the limo, but what you want is someone who will take the bus with you when the limo breaks down.

—OPRAH WINFREY

Below are some definitions of *Mate*:

1. A friend, buddy, or comrade
2. One of a pair
3. A spouse, partner, boyfriend, or girlfriend
4. Nautical: an on-deck naval officer who keeps watch and ensures the safety and security of the vessel. The captain relies heavily on the first and second mates in his stead.
5. *Wheel House*: Those who see and support you and your mission. The fourth and final step of the Wheel House Foundation is to choose and only allow into your life and home the friends, partners, family, and colleagues who look out for your best interests and support you on your quest to be the best you, offering your unique gifts to the world.

When we think of the word *Mate*, we often think about a marriage or life partner. Let's expand that vision to include anyone who has your back—your BFF, your buddy, your roommate, or even your four-legged companion. After all, Adam had Eve, Lucy had Desi, Laverne had Shirley, and Shaggy had Scooby.

Only after first taking the time to figure out who you are will you be ready to have a true Mate and partner. Many young people rush into relationships without fully developing themselves. As they continue to grow and learn through experience, the partnership can fall apart due to incompatibility. The allure of a big wedding, societal influences, parental expectations, and the sometimes-not-so-gentle push for a ring can pressure a couple into a premature commitment.

So many people I've talked to have had serious regrets even as they walked down the aisle. While looking into the eyes of their betrothed, they had serious doubts and a pounding heart as the minister asked them to recite the vows that would bind them for life. Once the honeymoon phase ends, sometimes they are stuck, not truly knowing themselves and with a partner who unknowingly isn't a match.

What if we adopted a new perspective where people, young and old, took the time to understand how they were made, what their triggers and interests are, and who would complement their personality perfectly? That would be for our primary relationship.

To continue building our pack of supporters, consider Esther Perel's words: "Today we turn to one person to provide what an entire village once did: a sense of grounding, meaning, and continuity."[18] Your next step in the Wheel House Method process is to build friendships that can fulfill other aspects of a caring relationship, enhance your life, and provide support.

That brings us to friendships. To lessen the strain on our primary relationships, should we choose to have one, we must have friends who truly get us and love us unconditionally. According to the article "The 13 Essential Traits of Good Friends" in *Psychology Today*, good friends possess thirteen qualities:

- Trustworthiness
- Honesty

- Dependability
- Loyalty
- Trusts others
- Empathetic
- Nonjudgmental
- Good listener
- Supportive in good times
- Supportive in bad times
- Self-confident
- Sees the humor in life
- Fun to be around[19]

There are several things to consider when searching for true friendships. True friends are not just social media connections or people who talk behind your back. They aren't fair-weather, overly competitive, or dishonest. Instead, they support you in good times and bad, show up for important occasions, and sit with you when you are having a hard time. They don't give unsolicited advice, they are honest even when it risks discomfort, and they never gossip about you. True friends make amends when they hurt you, talk things through, invite you to meet other friends, laugh at your jokes, cry with you, and offer unconditional love.

Without a solid support system of primary and secondary relationships, you will feel an emptiness in your heart. You may try to fill this with food, alcohol, social media, one-night stands, constant activity, work, drugs, superficial relationships, and more. Yet late at night in your home, the real you will be lonely until you put on your public face again.

Create a welcoming space in your home for friends and family to gather—a fire pit, a spacious kitchen counter, a sports court, an amazing basement to watch football or play cards, a sunroom for afternoon visits, or a cozy front porch to sit for a while. Let those characteristics express the real you and invite people over to share.

It doesn't have to be perfect. Embrace that pop-in visit, even if there's unfolded laundry on the couch or a dead house plant you haven't tossed . Let your real self shine. You'll be surprised how relieved people feel without the pressure to be perfect.

When I think about the Mates in my life, I realize I've been intentional about surrounding myself with people who don't just show up for the highlight reel; they show up for the real story.

Take the Sippin' Sistas. They are my work friends who have become so much more than networking contacts. They support every wild idea I have—the podcast launch, the book, the evolution of the Wheel House Method. But more importantly, they support *me*. They're the ones who remind me who I am when I get too caught up in what I'm building. They celebrate the wins and talk me through the setbacks with equal enthusiasm and honesty.

Then there are the Ya-Yas—the women I wrote about in my essay for *The Oprah Winfrey Show*, and honestly, that piece barely scratched the surface of what those friendships mean to me. We've been through decades together now, navigating life's ups and downs, celebrating each other's victories, and holding each other through losses. These are the friends who knew me before I became "Kim Costa, Top

5% real estate agent." They knew me when I was still figuring out who I wanted to be. And they're still here, cheering me on, keeping me grounded, reminding me that success means nothing if you don't have people to share it with.

There are also many creative friends I've bonded with as I have further developed my innate right-brainedness. They are the kind of people who just get how I'm made as a creative soul. I've found these friends to be pure joy as we develop our mission-driven messages together.

And then there's Rocky—my perfect Mate in every sense of the word. Our personalities don't match; they complement each other in the best possible way. Where I'm enthusiastic and expansive, he's steady and grounded. Our values align completely. We both believe in authenticity, in showing up fully, in building a life that matters. He doesn't just tolerate my ambitious vision; he champions it. He's my safe place, my sounding board, and my biggest supporter.

Add my kids who are the light of my life, Rocky's amazing kids, and our extended families to this mix and I have a network of Mates that makes everything else possible. They're a huge part of my foundation.

Here's what I've learned about the Mates area of the Wheel House: Quality trumps quantity every single time. It's not about having the most friends or the busiest social calendar. It's about cultivating relationships with people whose values align with yours, who challenge you to grow, who celebrate your authenticity, and who love you, not despite your imperfections but because they see your whole self and choose you anyway.

Part 4

THE WHEEL HOUSE ASSESSMENT

In this section, I will explain the Wheel House Assessment that combines questions based on Maslow's Hierarchy of Needs with the eight elements of the Wheel of Life. After discussing each area of the Wheel of Life, I'll share an example from my experience of living at Clarity Farm to highlight the most relevant reasons for my eventual move. I'll also include a client success story for each area to explain how this process might work and what success in each area might look like.

The questions for each of the eight Wheel of Life elements will prompt you to evaluate the current alignment of each area of your home. Different people in the home may have varying perspectives on how well the current home fits their desired lifestyle in each area. Discussing these differences can be mutually beneficial as you move forward to make compromises and consider each other's needs while planning your ideal home together.

Chapter by chapter, we will use a set of questions for each area of the Wheel of Life, arranged in ascending order according to Maslow's hierarchy, to measure your current living situation against your ideal lifestyle. This process is designed to guide you through the hierarchy, evaluating and grading your home in each area.

Once you evaluate all eight areas and grade each area using the Wheel House Assessment tool, you will have a snapshot of your overall home satisfaction and identify which areas need improvement. At this time, you can develop a plan of action with your real estate agent or interior designer to enhance your life through your home. That might involve selling your current home, undertaking a remodel, or, if you're lucky, realizing that your home is already the best place for you.

In summary, as your life changes, so should your home. As your home evolves, so does your life. You can revisit this process whenever your goals or life circumstances shift.

Focus on the explanations in the eight Wheel of Life areas and complete the Wheel House Assessment chapter by chapter, one section at a time. This process can be completed in just a few days, if necessary.

Then you (and anyone else involved in the decision-making process) will be armed and ready with the Wheel House Assessment results. Please share these results with your real estate agent or contact me at LifestyleFoundations.com to facilitate this process that will create a clarified overview of your findings and connect you to a qualified real estate agent and local expert in your search area.

This tool is not only great for assessing how your current home works for each individual but also for uncovering areas for improvement and seeking solutions and compromises to enhance everyone's future living situation. Taking the Wheel House Assessment will open up opportunities for conversation with your real estate agent, interior designer, partner, and others living in the home. Consider this the brainstorming phase of the process to bring all ideas and truths together. With the help of a qualified professional, you can sift through them to find the best outcome for everyone.

Read through each section of questions and jot down specific answers as you go. Pay attention to how strongly you feel when you evaluate your answers to the prompts at the end of each section. Rate your current home from 1 to 10 (with 10 being the highest) based on how well it fulfills your wants and needs in that area.

If a question is a deal-breaker for you in any area, rate that section of the Wheel of Life a zero. For example, the Friends and Family section of the questionnaire asks if you are expecting any additions to the family. If you and your partner are expecting a new baby but your current home only has one bedroom, that's probably a deal-breaker. Having the baby in your room indefinitely isn't feasible, and there is no way to add on to your high-rise condo.

Even if every other answer is a 10, that section would get 0 out of 10 because you are not willing to stay there for that one reason. Note that you have already decided to go, or move, and yet it is helpful to review the other answers. All your wants need to be considered when seeking alignment with your ideal home. For a free downloadable version to record your Wheel House Assessment results, visit *liveinyourwheelhousebook.com/resources*.

Wheel House Assessment

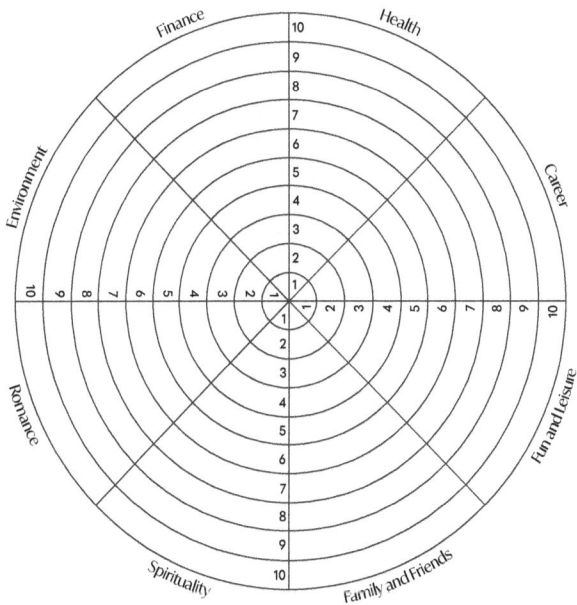

Wheel House Assessment Notes

Health (Mental and Physical)

Career and Job

Fun and Leisure

Family and Friends

Spirituality and Growth

Romance (Partner and Love)

Environment (Geography, Climate, etc)

Finance (Wealth and Money)

Chapter 15

HEALTH

*It is health that is real wealth
and not pieces of gold and silver.*

—MAHATMA GANDHI

Home is where we store and prepare our food. *Is it junk food or nourishing food?* It's where we rest. *Is it quality rest?* It's where we nourish our souls. *Do we have space to imagine and refuel?* It's where we unpack our worries and feel our deepest feelings. *Are we safe to express ourselves in our homes?*

Living a healthy lifestyle can lead to a longer life. Creating healthy habits at home is vital to our overall well-being. New research from the American Cancer Society shows that adults who follow the five healthy lifestyle habits below may live over a decade longer than those who don't.

- Eating a healthy diet
- Getting regular exercise
- Not smoking
- Maintaining a healthy weight
- Limiting alcohol[20]

In the same study, researchers noted that despite the United States being one of the wealthiest countries and spending more per capita on health care than any other nation, we rank thirty-first in average life expectancy. The American Cancer Society article explains, "According to the authors, the US healthcare system focuses mainly on drug discovery and disease management, even though a greater emphasis on prevention could go a long way toward controlling the most common and most expensive diseases, including cancer and cardiovascular disease."[21]

Health equals happiness. As reported by Consumer Affairs, a University of Kent and University of Reading study polled over 40,000 households in the United Kingdom and revealed how sticking to healthy habits can improve consumers' moods. Participants who exercised regularly and ate a diet full of fruits and vegetables were notably the happiest.[22]

Where can prevention and planning for a healthy lifestyle begin? At home. Success is more about building healthy habits than relying on willpower. An article in the *New York Times* summarizes that starting with lofty health goals is less effective than taking small steps over time to increase our health.[23] For those of us who have killed ourselves at the gym and ended up sore for a week, this is a welcome relief.

Tiny habits yield significant results. B. J. Fogg, author of *Tiny Habits*, has a proven system for lasting health improvements.

1. **Start small:** A short daily walk may lead to an exercise habit. Swapping chips for fruit at lunch can lead to a healthier diet.
2. **Do it every day:** The median time to create a new habit is sixty-six days. Habits form faster with daily practice.
3. **Make it easy:** Remove obstacles by cleaning out your pantry for only healthy choices or putting on gym clothes first thing in the morning. Even better, sleep in those clothes and roll out of bed onto the treadmill.
4. **Reward yourself:** Rewards reinforce habit formation. Plan a fun exercise date with a friend, listen to your favorite podcast while walking, or cook a healthy meal while watching your favorite show. HGTV, anyone?[24]

So how can your home support a healthy lifestyle? Access to nearby clean, nutritious food sources is key. Having parks, gyms, and other fitness providers within walking or driving distance can also be helpful. The quality of healthcare in your area significantly impacts your overall health. Accessible mental health care providers are increasingly vital to the well-being of all family members.

You can improve your mental health in your home by minimizing clutter, maximizing natural light, incorporating calming design elements, and designating spaces for relaxation and creative activities. A tidy, well-lit, nature-filled environment can reduce stress and anxiety, while a calming space or wellness nook can foster peace and rejuvenation. Engaging in hobbies at home, practicing self-care rituals, and connecting with nature indoors promote emotional well-being and a sense of control.

Another important consideration regarding your home as it relates to health is any inherent safety issues or physical limitations (e.g., mobility issues) of the owner that prevent ongoing maintenance or enjoyment of the home. As we discussed in Chapter 14, "Mate(s)," the people who live in or visit your home also affect your mental health.

At Clarity Farm, there were several health-related reasons why the home was not ideal. Yes, it had fresh air, room to roam, beautiful scenery, a craft room, and plenty of opportunities for clean living, including organic herbs and veggies. It had a cutting garden, a pool to swim in, horses to look at, and plenty of room for a home gym. Sounds good, right? But everywhere we needed to be was at least an hour's drive away, including school, church, doctors' appointments, work, groceries, and the list goes on and on.

So instead of living on the farm, I ended up "living" in my car. In fact, I even bought a conversion van because I felt so bad that my young son had to be away from home so much. At least he could nap comfortably in the van while we were out and about. It was exhausting. And more than once he asked, "Can we just go home?"

Another factor affecting this extrovert's health was the remoteness. If I worked from home, which I often did to save myself the hour-and-a-half drive to our family construction business, I saw no other people. My beautiful office near the front door and the wrap-around porch overlooking the enchanting valley adjoining the Little River was so lovely, and yet I longed for connection. I was lonely in my beautiful castle on the hill.

Finally, and most importantly, besides my broken back and the inability to ride horses, part of the reason I wanted to move to the farm in the first place was that my daughter was born with a rare neurological spinal cord condition that was worsening. After her initial spinal surgery at six weeks old, I had to watch her like a hawk until she stopped growing, staying vigilant for any worsening condition that would look like increasing loss of sensation, flexibility, or strength in her legs. I thought riding horses would strengthen her limbs and improve mobility during this battle. She also loved taking care of the horses.

After I broke my back, I often made my way to the riding ring on the back acreage to watch my daughter ride with her trainer. It was beautiful, and it was something she loved. I started noticing that her right foot would get jammed in the stirrup with her toes pointing down, a sign of increasing weakness in that leg.

Anyone who rides knows you must keep your heels down and behind the stirrup, and your toes up in front so if you fall or get bucked, your foot is not stuck in the stirrup with the possibility of getting dragged.

One day my daughter's slightly naughty horse, Avery, decided to rear in the same spot where I had broken my back. I almost passed out with fear as my daughter fell to the ground with a thud.

It was all overwhelming—physically and mentally. Despite all the wonderful things about Clarity Farm, it was going to be impossible to live in a place that no longer held the promise of health and vitality.

So after giving it a good try for many years, I knew I could not thrive there. I was unable to properly take care of the farm, I felt isolated and feared for my daughter's safety, realizing the certainty of impending further neurosurgeries for her spinal condition. I knew we had to go.

Looking back, Health was a 0 or 1 for me on the Wheel House Assessment at Clarity Farm. It was time to move to a place with the promise of less driving, less maintenance, more time for other hobbies, and a greater connection for mental and physical health.

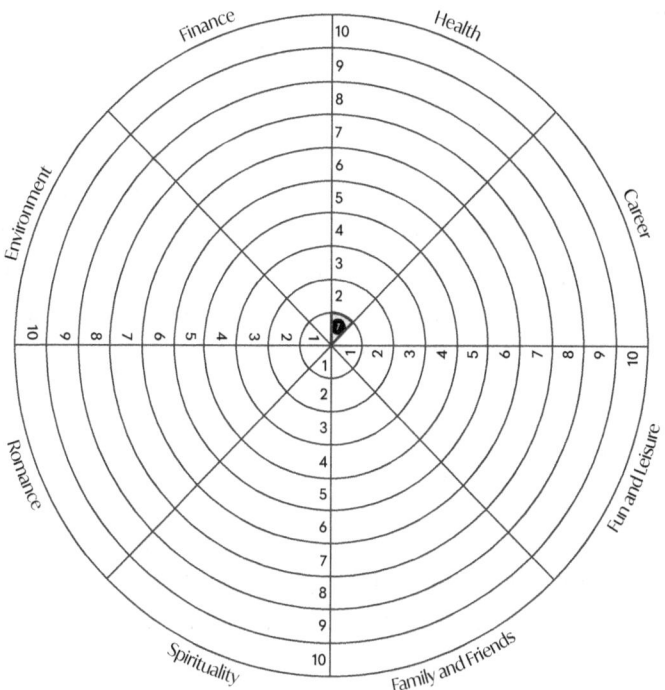

Wheel House Success Story

Lucy's Health Transformation

Before

Lucy, in her 60s, was living in what she jokingly called her "urban obstacle course." Her charming old city building had more mold than a blue cheese factory, and just getting to her kitchen required climbing two steep sets of stairs that felt more like Mount Everest, thanks to her arthritis. Add the traffic, the crime in her neighborhood, and her growing fear of going outside, and Lucy found herself retreating into isolation. Her home, instead of being a place of rest, was draining her physically and mentally.

The Shift

Walking through Lucy's Wheel House health questions helped her see what was really happening. Her environment wasn't supporting her well-being. It wasn't her slowing down; it was her home dragging her down. Once she let go of the idea that she had to tough it out, she realized a safer, healthier, and more joyful lifestyle was possible without giving up independence.

After

Lucy traded her moldy stair marathon for a small, newer cottage in the outer suburbs. Her new home has a bedroom just for her and an office where she can work remotely, no stair climbing required. Down the street is a park where she walks daily, and she even joined a tennis league that reconnected her with friends (and her sense of humor). The cleaner air and lower crime rates give her peace of mind, and for the first time in years, she feels safe enough to step outside and explore what she enjoys. Lucy laughs that her "doctor prescribed a house move," and it worked better than any medication.

Now it's time for you to assess your current home versus your ideal home in Health on the Wheel House Assessment. Grab your Wheel House Assessment worksheet and write notes regarding your thoughts after considering the following questions and any additional findings in the area of Health that may not be addressed here. The questions are arranged in an advancing sequence starting from the lower needs to the higher needs of Maslow's Hierarchy of Needs. Remember to write any notes that stand out on the second page of your worksheet as you read through the questions.

Health Questions

1. Physiological Needs (basic survival: air, water, shelter, food, sleep)
- Does the home have draftiness, water, lead, radon, or mold issues that affect comfort and health?
- Is your home well-lit with adequate natural light during the day?
- Do you live in a cold region, and is the home adequately insulated and heated?
- Is quality, healthy food (including organic options) available close by?
- Is the water quality safe for drinking and cooking (tap, well, or filtered)?
- Does the home provide adequate ventilation and indoor air quality (HVAC, fresh air flow)?
- Does the home support healthy sleep (quiet rooms, soundproofing, darkness at night)?

2. Safety Needs (security, stability, protection, accessibility)
- Can you maintain your home physically (upkeep, chores)?

- Can you climb the stairs safely, or does the home need accessibility features (ramps, rails, lifts)?
- Do you live with anyone who is abusive or unsafe?
- Is adequate health care located close to your home?
- Do you have health issues that impact your home life?
- Does the home have smoke detectors, carbon monoxide detectors, and fire extinguishers?
- Is there reliable pest control (termites, rodents, insects) to prevent health risks?
- Are emergency response times (fire, EMS, police) adequate in your area?

3. Love and Belonging (connection, family, social wellness)
- Does the home provide spaces that foster family meals, connection, and shared activities?
- Does the neighborhood and community offer social or wellness groups (walking clubs, recreation leagues, fitness classes)?

4. Esteem Needs (confidence, accomplishment, independence)
- Are you able to work out at home? Or is it easy to exercise close to your home (gym, trails, etc.)?
- Do you have access to the sports and exercise you enjoy (yoga, tennis, golf, hiking, etc.)?
- Does the home support your wellness routines (quiet meditation space, workout corner, standing desk)?

5. Cognitive Needs (knowledge, meaning, exploration, growth)
   - If desired, do you have access to massage, nutrition, acupuncture, and other holistic health services?
   - Is there space in the home that encourages learning about health (a library, an office, a media setup)?
   - Do you have access to reliable technology and private space for telehealth or online wellness programs?
   - Are there health initiatives in your community where you can receive instruction and support on improving your health?

6. Aesthetic Needs (beauty, harmony, restorative design)
   - Is seasonal weather affecting your physical or emotional well-being?
   - Does your home's design and layout create a sense of calm, relaxation, or healing?
   - Does your yard, balcony, or nearby nature provide beauty and restorative views?
   - Are elements of nature that promote peace and serenity incorporated into your home's decor?

7. Self-Actualization (personal fulfillment, optimal wellness, living with purpose)
   - Does your home inspire you to prioritize long-term wellness goals (training for a race, daily yoga, gardening for nutrition)?

- Does your environment encourage personal rituals (morning stretches, meditation, journaling) that optimize your health and growth?
- Does your home environment align with the life you're meant to live and support your highest potential?

Now that you have completed the Wheel House Assessment section of Health and reviewed your answers, before you move on to the next section, shade in your score from 1–10 in the Health section on the Wheel House Assessment pie chart. Then highlight any significant findings you have written down, either good or bad, in the notes section. These findings from all parties involved will help you decide whether to rearrange areas of your home or discuss potential relocation or renovation plans with your local agent, designer, or contractor.

Chapter 16

CAREER

I believe that being successful means having a balance of success stories across the many areas of your life. You can't truly be successful in your business life if your home life is in shambles.

—ZIG ZIGLAR

Career is the next lifestyle area in the Wheel of Life. A move often becomes inevitable due to a promotion or other job change to a position based in another physical location.

For example, if someone had a job in Seattle, Washington, and accepted a new position in Charlotte, North Carolina, it would most likely require the selling and buying of a home. That would be a clear-cut example of a move made primarily for career reasons.. To lessen the effects on the commute, the family, and the finances, the hiring company's relocation department often pays many, if not all, of the moving expenses. On the Wheel House scale for Career, the homeowner might score 0 or 1 for how the current home meets the criteria for advancing their career. They will not have a career in their chosen job if they don't move to the new location.

Another example of moving for career reasons is when the homeowner lacks adequate workspace for a work-from-home job. Imagine a dual-income couple with three kids living in an open-concept home without dedicated spaces for either parent's work. One partner does paperwork on the kitchen counter and must clean it up every night before dinner. The other partner tries to complete Zoom calls from the living room as the dog barks and the kids run noisily through the home after school. It's not an ideal situation for either partner. They might rate their home a 2 or 3 out of 10 in the Career area.

Can they remodel to fix those issues? For example, can they turn the living room into an office or build another office in the basement? Or will they have to move to a new home to get any career-based work done in the house?

All they know is that with such a low score in Career, they cannot continue to feel consistently scattered and displaced, or to look unprofessional on video work calls and still be successful at their job. With their work interrupted and disorganized, the at-home work setup jeopardizes their careers (not to mention their family time). In this scenario, there isn't enough space in the home's current configuration for both family life and dual careers to be compatible.

In other situations, the decision to move for career reasons is not as straightforward. Workers' shifting priorities, especially after the 2019–2020 COVID pandemic, led to many changes in work-from-home statuses. Due to the rise in mental health initiatives, increasing financial concerns, and a renewed focus on employee retention, numerous independent studies have investigated the impact of working from home on career satisfaction and productivity. Both employers and employees have been seeking clarity as they navigate this new work-from-home frontier.

According to a March 2023 Pew Research Center report, 35 percent of US workers would choose to work from home full-time if they had the option, and another 41 percent would choose a hybrid work model.[25] In both instances, after working from home, these workers said they preferred their at-home work environment.

As work-from-home accommodations have risen, there has been a proliferation of studies on work-from-home productivity. Great Place to Work's two-year survey of 800,000 workers shows that productivity increased by over 6 percent when workers switched to remote work.[26] Increased productivity and higher satisfaction suggest that work-from-home accommodations are here to stay, at least for the financial, entrepreneurial, marketing, and consulting sectors.

Today's workforce highly values flexibility. Many employers are offering work-from-home options, if possible, to attract and retain the best employees. In the housing market, that means preexisting homes need to be modified to accommodate home offices, and new homes with one or two flex spaces must accommodate work-from-home owners.

There are other aspects to consider in the lifestyle element of Career. As more women have entered the workforce over the past few decades, there has been a growing sentiment that being a Super Woman (or Super Human, for that matter) is not possible. For many, the days are gone when one partner worked full-time and the other stayed home to care for the children and run the household. These demographic work-life changes have impacted not only workers in dual-income families but also their partners who now have more household and childcare responsibilities and work duties.

Another trend we are observing is people working later into their retirement years. According to a 2022 Gallup study, except for 2021, the average retirement age has increased steadily since the 1990s. It rose from an expected retirement age of 57 in 1991 to age 66 in 2022.[27]

The impact of these trends is that more people are juggling work and home life as they work longer, have more than one working person in a family, or work from home. There has never been a better time to evaluate whether your home supports your work life (and offers an escape) and whether your work reflects your values and talents to their fullest potential.

During the years I lived at Clarity Farm, along with being a mom, wife, and homemaker, I also worked as the accounting and human resources manager for our successful small residential construction business. Although I had a degree in marketing and sales management and was pursuing my master's degree in human resource development and a Certificate of Interior Design, I found myself stuck in tasks such as reconciling bank statements, completing workers' compensation audits, running payroll, and managing 401(k)s. My proclivity toward more extroverted, right-brained (intuitive, creative, and subjective) work was being overlooked in place of performing more left-brained (logical, analytical, and objective) work.

I often found myself working from my remote home office to avoid the hour-plus drive to our company's headquarters. I didn't have time to make the commute, get everything done, and then pick up the kids from school. As an extrovert, I found that time spent alone on tasks I was not suited for or inclined to choose was unfulfilling. I found my head aching as I repeated general ledger and QuickBooks entries ad nauseam.

Although our little company was very successful and created stunning luxury exterior environments for lovely clients, the specific role I had in that company was unsatisfying and draining. I would have scored a 2 in Career at that time.

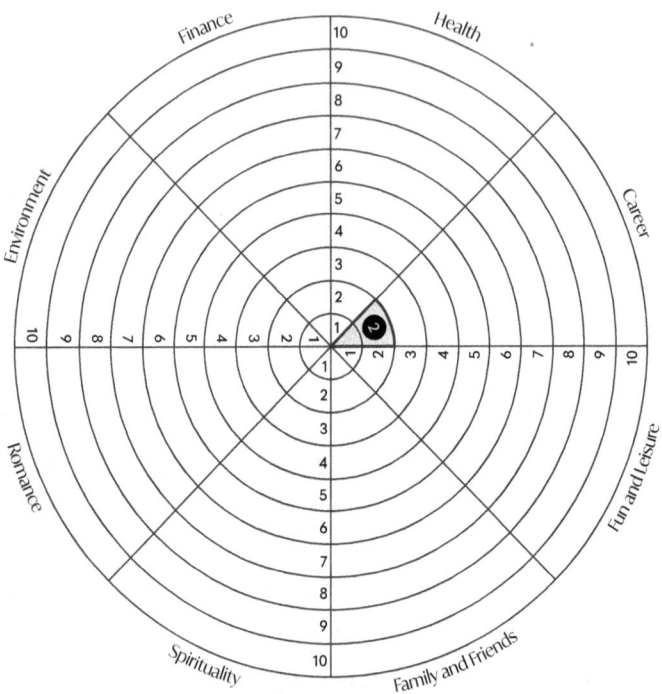

Wheel House Success Story

Thomas and Patti's Career Transformation

Before

Thomas and Patti were the definition of a power couple—two executives with demanding jobs, frequent travel schedules, and a family to raise. Their home, however, hadn't gotten the memo. With no real home offices to speak of, Patti (a technical writer) often found herself working from the kitchen table. Her papers had to be cleared away for dinner, which meant her train of thought derailed as frequently as the family's toy trains in the living room. Meanwhile, Thomas needed space for calls and strategy sessions, but household noise was a constant background track. Add to this the fact that they lived far from the airport (a nightmare for two frequent flyers), and their au pair had no proper space of her own. The family's daily rhythm was more chaos than balance.

The Shift

As they navigated their Wheel House Career questions, Thomas and Patti realized their home wasn't just inconvenient; it was actively holding them back. Their careers required focus, flexibility, and proximity to travel hubs, while their family needed both structure and support. The solution wasn't trying harder to make it work but finding a home that worked *for* them.

After

Thomas and Patti sold their ill-fitting house and found a new one close to their headquarters and the airport. That home had everything their careers and family life demanded: two private offices, a finished basement perfect for the au pair, and ample parking for a busy household. Now they work from home without juggling noise, space, or misplaced papers. Even better, the family has common areas designed for togetherness without bleeding into work zones. Patti jokes that she hasn't lost a thought to the clatter of silverware in months, and Thomas swears the shorter commute to the airport has added years back to his life.

Now it's time for you to assess your current home versus your ideal home in Career on the Wheel House Assessment. Grab your Wheel House Assessment worksheet and write notes regarding your thoughts after considering the following questions and any other scenarios relevant to you in the area of Career. As you read through the Career questions, remember to write any notes that stand out on the corresponding area for Career on the second page of your worksheet.

Career Questions

1. Physiological Needs (basic tools and workspace)
- Do you have a dedicated home office or workspace that meets your needs?
- Do you need more than one office or study space in your home?
- Do you have high-speed internet and the technology necessary to work effectively from home?
- Do you have adequate storage for work-related materials, tools, or supplies?

2. Safety Needs (stability, security, resources)
- Do you live close enough to your work, or is the commute too far?
- Is your neighborhood and town conducive to your career (access to clients, trade networks, resources)?

- Do you feel secure in your current job, or are you expecting a transfer or career change?
- Does your home provide a distraction-free environment for work (noise, kids, pets, etc.)?

3. Love and Belonging (connection, teamwork, relationships)
- Does your home environment support connection with coworkers or clients (hosting meetings, virtual calls)?
- Does your city or community provide networking opportunities and professional support groups?
- If you work from home, does your setup allow you to still feel socially connected?
- Does your location allow you to balance family, social, and work life effectively?

4. Esteem Needs (confidence, pride, achievement)
- Does your home workspace make you feel productive and professional?
- Do you feel proud of where you live when clients, colleagues, or peers visit (virtually or in person)?
- Does your city or area align with your professional identity and ambitions?
- Does your home environment support both your creative (right-brain) and logical (left-brain) needs?

5. Cognitive Needs (growth, awareness, learning)
- Are you in the right career, or do you want to switch jobs?

- Does your home environment give you space to learn, study, or develop new skills?
- Do you have access to educational or professional growth resources nearby (libraries, universities, training)?
- Does your environment inspire innovation and fresh thinking?

6. Aesthetic Needs (harmony, inspiration, motivation)
- Is your workspace visually appealing and energizing for productivity?
- Does the layout of your home separate work from relaxation, giving balance?
- Does your environment encourage creativity and focus?
- Is there natural light, design, or order in your workspace that inspires you?

7. Self-Actualization (purpose, fulfillment, calling)
- Does your home environment support you in pursuing your career purpose and passions?
- Does your career align with the lifestyle you want your home to provide?
- Does your home give you flexibility to adapt as your career evolves (remote work, business growth, retirement)?
- Does your career environment empower you to make a greater contribution to your field or community?

Now that you have completed the Wheel House Assessment section of Career and reviewed your answers, before you move on to the next section, shade in your score from 1–10 in the Career section on the Wheel House Assessment pie chart. Then highlight any significant findings, either good or bad, in the note section for the area of Career on your Wheel House Assessment worksheet. These findings will be helpful as you rearrange areas of your home or discuss your potential relocation or renovation plans with your local agent, designer, or contractor.

Chapter 17

FUN AND LEISURE

Enjoy life. There's plenty of time to be dead.
—HANS CHRISTIAN ANDERSEN

Palliative nurse Bronnie Ware stated in her book *The Top Five Regrets of the Dying* that a common phrase she heard was that "no one on their deathbed ever said, I wish I had spent more time at work."[28] I would add the exception of being in your dream career, surrounded by fun and supportive people, and fulfilling your life's mission. Whether entertaining in your home or traveling the world to achieve your mission, the fun and connection you did or didn't have in life is what you will remember on your deathbed.

It might be holidays, birthdays, cookouts, baby showers, intimate dinners, movie screenings, barbecues by the pool, garden parties, book clubs, Bible studies, Super Bowl parties—the list goes on and on. If well-planned, they all have some things in common. They bring together loved ones in your home (which should reflect the authentic you); spotlight a favorite pastime, season, or celebration; and provide a venue for self-expression, relaxation, and gratitude for you and your guests. These special events are opportunities for connection and joy to come alive in your home. As Barbara Hall deftly said on the TV show *Northern Exposure*, "That's the secret of entertaining. You make your guests feel welcome in your home. If you do that honestly, the rest takes care of itself."[29]

But entertaining is just one flavor of fun. Your home should be the launchpad for joy in all its forms. Maybe it's game nights that stretch past midnight, movie marathons in pajamas, or backyard camping adventures that let your kids feel like explorers without leaving home.

Perhaps you're the one who hosts spontaneous pizza parties, weekend brunch gatherings where mimosas flow as freely as conversation, or elegant dinner parties that make any night feel like a celebration. Your home might be command central for book club meetings, craft nights with friends, or football watch parties that turn your basement into the neighborhood tavern.

Or maybe you're an empty nester finally claiming space for that pottery wheel you've always wanted. Or perhaps you're a single professional who has transformed a spare room into the ultimate vinyl listening lounge.

And let's not forget the everyday fun—the kitchen dance parties while cooking dinner, the living room fort-building sessions, the front porch sunset-watching that becomes your unwinding ritual, or the Saturday mornings spent mastering sourdough just because you can.

But leisure matters just as much as fun. Your home should also be your sanctuary for genuine rest and restoration—the place where you can curl up with a novel in your favorite reading nook, practice yoga in a quiet corner flooded with morning light, or simply sit in your garden and do absolutely nothing. It's where you might lose yourself in a hobby, whether it's painting in a sunlit studio space, tending plants on your balcony, or tinkering in the garage on projects that feed your soul.

And here's another truth: The right home doesn't just create space for fun within its walls; it connects you to a community where fun flourishes. When you're close to walking trails, neighborhood parks, local festivals, farmers' markets, and downtown gathering spots, your home becomes the base camp for adventures that extend beyond your property line.

It's the place you leave for morning coffee runs that turn into sidewalk conversations, weekend concerts in the park, or spontaneous trips to that ice cream shop everyone loves. When your home is designed with both fun and leisure in mind—whether that means a cozy media room, a kitchen island built for cooking together, outdoor spaces that beg you to linger, quiet retreats that invite you to pause and breathe, or a location that puts you at the heart of community life—it naturally becomes the place where memories get made and spirits get restored.

The best homes don't just shelter us; they invite us to play, connect, rest, explore, and remember that life is meant to be enjoyed, not just endured. Exposing yourself to new possibilities for fun will heighten your mood and present many opportunities for exploration, friendship, and learning. Make fun, leisure, and entertainment a regular part of your life and set up your home to bring the most joy.

Even though I have always been a golfer, I decided at Clarity Farm to try my hand at horseback riding and running a horse farm. I even ran the local Pony Club. While I met some amazing people and still admire equestrians and the horses, I was not cut out to be an equestrian. In fact, it just about crippled me.

I like to travel, but I couldn't do so easily when there were animals to take care of. I wanted to entertain—that was fun at the farm. People loved it, but it was a lot of work to get everything just right on that big property. I loved crafts, reading, and writing, but with all the maintenance and commuting involved with the farm, I had no time for them. I even bought a hammock that I could see from the kitchen window, dreaming of just relaxing and hearing all the nature sounds, but I don't think I ever actually lay in that hammock. I was too busy doing everything to keep up the farm and travel to and from it.

And the community engagement that I enjoy so much was just too far away. I could barely see any neighbors, let alone have a casual conversation while out on a walk. There were a lot of quiet, casual nights with wholesome activities, music nights with the kids, playing games in the pool, cookouts, and birthday parties on the farm. We really did enjoy sharing our farm with our loved ones.

I would score Fun and Leisure a 4. The fun part of having everyone at the farm was significant. But there was very little leisure time, and I was doing much of the maintenance and pursuing all the wrong hobbies.

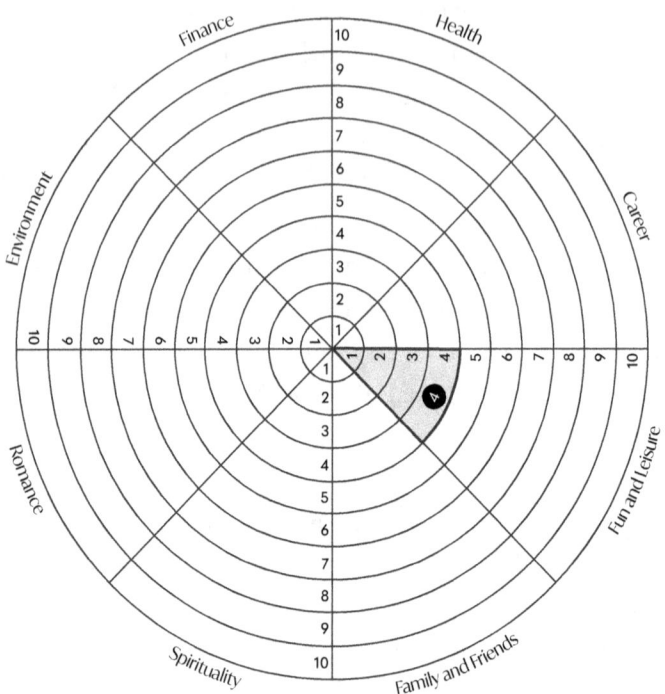

Wheel House Success Story

Paul's Fun and Leisure Transformation

Before

Paul, a man in his fifties, had been living in the same swim and tennis neighborhood since his divorce fifteen years earlier. Back then, the house made sense; it was the family hub. But with his kids grown and gone, Paul found himself rattling around in a house built for a life he no longer had. Weekends were too quiet. His neighbors were busy grilling out with kids and grandkids, and he couldn't help but feel a twinge of jealousy (and maybe a little boredom) as he pushed a mower across his oversized lawn. His home had become less a source of joy and more a reminder of deferred maintenance and deferred fun.

The Shift

When Paul considered his Wheel House Fun and Leisure questions, it hit him. He wasn't stuck; he was living in a house that no longer fit his current chapter of life. The home that once served his family so well was now keeping him tethered to chores and memories instead of possibilities. What he really craved was freedom, connection, and adventure.

After

Paul sold the memory-filled, maintenance-heavy family home and moved into a sleek new place downtown. Now he could walk to restaurants, meet friends on a whim, and skip the endless yard work, thanks to an HOA that handled the exterior. Even better, the lock-and-leave setup gave him freedom to travel. Instead of watching neighbors have fun, Paul was the one posting vacation photos and texting friends to meet him for dinner. He jokes that he traded in his lawn mower for a suitcase and doesn't miss the grass one bit.

Now it's time for you to assess your current home versus your ideal home's score in Fun and Leisure on the Wheel House Assessment. Grab your Wheel House Assessment worksheet and write notes regarding your thoughts after considering the following questions and any other areas of Fun and Leisure you'd like to add that are important to you.

The questions are arranged in an advancing sequence starting from the lower needs to the higher needs of Maslow's Hierarchy of Needs. Remember to write any notes that stand out on the corresponding area for Fun and Leisure on the second page of your worksheet as you read through the Fun and Leisure questions.

Fun and Leisure Questions

1. Physiological Needs (basic enjoyment, comfort)
- Do you have enough space to watch TV, movies, or play games?
- Do you have high-speed internet and Wi-Fi to support your leisure activities?
- Does your home have a yard, a pool, a sports court, or other play areas for family and friends?
- Do you have enough space in your home for family members to entertain friends at the same time?

2. Safety Needs (accessibility, ease, logistics)
- Is there adequate parking for guests when you entertain?
- Is your kitchen functional and large enough for cooking and social gatherings?
- Is your home designed to accommodate larger gatherings (holidays, parties) safely?
- Do you feel your community is safe and accessible for recreational activities (parks, sports, nightlife)?

3. Love and Belonging (connection, shared fun, community)
   - Do you have spaces to host and connect with friends and family (indoors and outdoors)?
   - Are there enough seating and gathering areas for holidays, parties, or casual get-togethers?
   - Do you live in a community where neighbors and friends enjoy social or recreational activities together?
   - Are there local groups, clubs, or events that align with your hobbies and interests?

4. Esteem Needs (pride, status, fulfillment through leisure)
   - Does your home and yard allow you to host events you feel proud of (BBQs, holidays, birthdays)?
   - Do you feel proud of the recreational spaces your home provides (pool, pavilion, craft room, hobby space)?
   - Does your community's entertainment and leisure scene reflect your lifestyle (restaurants, arts, nightlife)?
   - Do you have a space that highlights your personal hobbies or passions (craft room, music studio, workshop)?

5. Cognitive Needs (growth, exploration, learning)
   - Are you located near cultural opportunities that expand your mind (museums, music venues, arts)?
   - Does your home provide space for creative hobbies and personal growth (crafts, music, reading)?

- Does your environment encourage exploration and discovery through leisure (trails, biking, travel)?
- Are you near an airport or a transportation hub so you can easily explore beyond your local area?

6. Aesthetic Needs (beauty, playfulness, design)
   - Does your home and yard feel inviting and inspiring for relaxation and play?
   - Do outdoor spaces (patio, garden, pool, pavilion) support beauty and enjoyment?
   - Is your leisure space visually appealing and conducive to creativity and fun?
   - Does your community provide attractive spaces to relax, play, and connect (parks, plazas, venues)?

7. Self-Actualization (joy, fulfillment, lifestyle alignment)
   - Does your home environment support the joy and fulfillment you want from leisure time?
   - Does your location allow you to pursue the hobbies, sports, and experiences that matter most to you?
   - Do your leisure spaces reflect your authentic self and the lifestyle you aspire to?
   - Does your home inspire you to balance work, play, and relaxation in ways that nurture your best life?

Now that you have completed the Wheel House Assessment section of Fun and Leisure and reviewed your answers, before you move on to the next section, shade in your score from 1–10 in the Fun and Leisure section on the Wheel House Assessment pie chart. Then highlight any significant findings, either good or bad, in the note section for the area of Fun and Leisure on your Wheel House Assessment worksheet. These findings will be helpful as you rearrange areas of your home or discuss your potential relocation or renovation plans with your local agent, designer, or contractor.

Chapter 18

FAMILY AND FRIENDS

Let us be grateful to the people who make us happy; they are the charming gardeners who make our souls blossom.

—MARCEL PROUST

What makes a house a home? More than the decorations, it's the people living with you and the people you invite in. A home is as cozy as the family and friends you have surrounding you.

Just picture a gathering around a holiday meal with the table set for family and a few close friends. Food is shared, toasts are given, and stories are told. Laughter fills the room, and new memories are made. This is the stuff that fills your home with coziness and lasting good vibes.

When you fill your home with people who know you and accept you for who you are, there is a feeling of peace. When you open your home to anyone, you invite them to come closer—to see and know you. In turn, they add variety to your life with their gifts, stories, food, and comforting presence.

There are specific ways a home can help or hinder your relationships with friends and family. For the immediate family, there is a balance of space and togetherness for everyone. Everyone's needs should be taken into consideration. From privacy to space for individual needs, family and friends are a primary consideration in your home.

Let's focus on extended friends and family and how they can influence where your home is and whom you invite over.

- Do your family and friends live in the same town, or will they need to stay overnight when they visit?
- Do you have convenient transportation available to your home?

- Do you have enough space for your family for dinner or other events?
- If not, can rooms be turned into entertaining areas to accommodate everyone?
- Is there enough parking close by for guests?
- Is the kitchen big enough for more than one cook?
- Do you have adequate storage space for food?
- Is your home child-proofed for young children?
- Does anyone who might be visiting regularly have physical limitations?
- Are there activities or interests your friends and family might enjoy nearby?
- Have you made them feel welcome in your home by displaying photos and doing little things to make them comfortable?

On the flip side, if things are not all rosy and you've had some conflict or loss with your extended family and close friends, feel unsafe, or feel as though you cannot be yourself, how do you position yourself in your home for peace and acceptance? Unfortunately, not every change in life is positive.

If you are considering a move for a fresh start, remember that wherever you go, there you are. In other words, your problems may follow you. Ensure you have given some time to pass after any serious conflict or loss. You will want to make a clear-headed decision in your best interests, possibly with guidance from a mental health professional. Grief is a process; give it time.

Know that change is a stressor. You may be making a change that allows for growth and happiness, but give it time to unfold once you arrive. It may take a year or two to settle into your new environment.

Examine many options and give them a trial run. Don't make a rushed or snap decision based on your current level of discomfort. Is reconciliation possible? Have you processed your grief and looked for the best solution for the future?

If you decide to move, hire a local real estate professional to help you uncover the ins and outs of any new area. They should be able to answer any questions about local laws, zoning, opportunities to explore your interests, and so on.

Take a complete inventory of what you want this family and friends' area of your life to look like. Do a deep dive into what the perfect home might offer to help make this area a fit for you.

If you are considering a lifestyle change due to your family and friends, you are not alone. Whether you want to move closer to and engage with your family more to increase all those good times or want a healthy, fresh start, there are options to help you be the best *you* with people who love and support you.

When we bought Clarity Farm, I thought I'd found the perfect escape—a sanctuary where we could build the kind of life I'd always dreamed of. And in many ways, it was. The property was stunning, the kind of place where you could host epic gatherings and create memories that would last a lifetime. Friends would visit and marvel at what we'd built. "This is like a resort," they said, and they weren't wrong.

But here's the thing about living on a resort: Someone has to maintain it, and that someone was us. I used to joke with my kids, "You can't just live on the resort—you have to help take care of the resort." They'd roll their eyes, but they knew I was serious. There were animals to feed, fences to mend, pastures and a pool to maintain. Entertaining was fun, but it was also a lot of work. And while we loved having people over, the reality was that Clarity Farm's remote location made spontaneous hangouts nearly impossible.

Distance became the double-edged sword of our lives there. On the one hand, we were blissfully far from certain family members whose drama we didn't need in our daily lives. On the other hand, we were too far from the friends and family we actually wanted to see more of. The people who filled our cups, who made life richer, required planning, coordination, and a willingness to drive down our long, winding driveway.

And then there was school. My kids were bright, curious, and qualified for TAG (Talented and Gifted) and other specialized programs that would challenge and engage them. But our private school and our local public school didn't offer those opportunities. The county next door did, though. So while Clarity Farm gave us space and beauty, it couldn't give my children the academic environment they deserved.

When I think back on our time there through the lens of Family and Friends, I'd give it a 4 out of 10. It wasn't a failure, but it wasn't thriving either. We had moments of connection and joy, but they came at a cost—effort, isolation, and trade-offs that eventually became too heavy to ignore.

Your home should bring the people you love closer, not require them to make a pilgrimage just to see you. It should support your children's growth, not limit their opportunities. And while a little distance from toxic relationships can be healthy, you shouldn't have to sacrifice proximity to the people who truly matter.

Clarity Farm taught me that even the most beautiful setting can't compensate for misalignment in the relationships that sustain us.

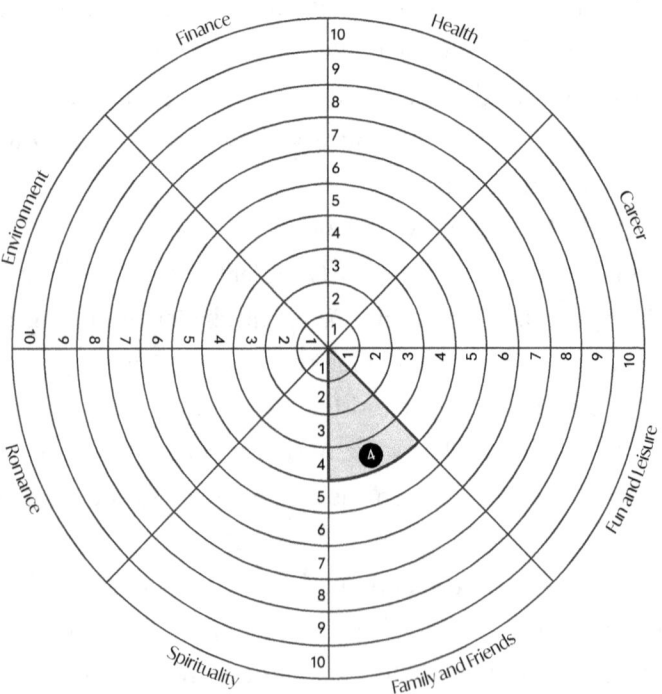

Wheel House Success Story
Stella and Sam's Family and Friends Transformation

Before

Stella and Sam loved their chic high-rise condo in the city. With two bedrooms, skyline views, and all the restaurants they could walk to, it was perfect when it was just the two of them and their toddler. But with another baby on the way, their sleek setup was starting to feel more like a shoebox. They dreamed of a yard where their kids (and maybe a dog) could run, but the reality was closer to tripping over toy trucks in the living room. On top of that, Stella planned to quit her job to stay home with the children, which would mean she'd need more support. Both sets of grandparents lived in the northern suburbs, a full hour away, which made pop-in babysitting more of a fantasy than a reality.

The Shift

As they navigated the Wheel House Family and Friends questions, Stella and Sam discovered what they had already known in their hearts: City living had been ideal for their twenties and early parenthood, but their family stage required something new. A bigger home in a community with strong schools and closer proximity to family would not only ease the pressure but also give them a sense of belonging and support as their children grew.

After

Stella and Sam moved into a four-bedroom home located halfway between both sets of grandparents who could swing by to help or even stay overnight when needed. The excellent school system gave them confidence about their kids' futures, and the neighborhood moms' group ensured that playdates—and adult company—were always nearby. Summers were filled with art and sports camps at the local park, giving the kids plenty of opportunities to make new friends. Stella and Sam laugh that their new home may not have the same skyline views, but it has something better: space for family, friends, and the kind of joyful chaos they actually want.

Now it's time for you to assess your current home versus your ideal home's score in Family and Friends on the Wheel House Assessment. Grab your Wheel House Assessment worksheet and write notes regarding your thoughts after considering the following questions and any other scenarios that might apply to you. Remember to write any notes that stand out on the corresponding area for Family and Friends on the second page of your worksheet as you read through the Family and Friends questions.

Family and Friends Questions

1. Physiological Needs (space, basics for household members)
   - Do you have enough bedrooms and bathrooms for everyone living in the home?

- Do you have space for overnight guests or visiting family?
- Is there enough kitchen and dining space to prepare and share meals?
- Do you have room to accommodate new family members (children, pets, au pair, etc.)?

2. Safety Needs (health, caregiving, stability)
- Do family or friends who live with you (or visit) have any medical needs or accessibility requirements that your home must meet?
- Is there room to care for an aging parent, older relative, or someone in transition (illness, divorce, loss)?
- Does your home allow everyone to feel safe, comfortable, and supported in their routines?
- Do pets and family members have the space and setup they need to thrive safely?

3. Love and Belonging (connection, closeness, community)
- Do you live close enough—or far enough—from family to maintain healthy relationships?
- Is your neighborhood socially welcoming and supportive of making new friends?
- Do you feel connected to your community (schools, neighbors, activities)?
- Do you have spaces at home that encourage togetherness (family dinners, shared activities, play areas)?

4. Esteem Needs (pride, hosting, family identity)
   - Do you have enough room for family functions, gatherings, or celebrations?
   - Do you enjoy hosting friends and family, and does your home support it (kitchen, living room, yard)?
   - Are you proud to invite family and friends into your home?
   - Do you feel your home reflects the personalities of the people who live there?

5. Cognitive Needs (awareness, transitions, planning)
   - Are you adding to the family, expecting children, or planning for changing household needs?
   - Are you new to the area and need a neighborhood that makes it easy to build friendships?
   - Are you prepared for potential transitions such as divorce, loss of a loved one, or an older relative moving in?
   - Do you have the flexibility in your home to adjust to changing family dynamics over time?

6. Aesthetic Needs (harmony, warmth, family feel)
   - Does your home feel warm, inviting, and welcoming for family and friends?
   - Is the space balanced—not so cramped that it feels stressful or so large that family members feel disconnected?

- Does the design of your home encourage family bonding (cozy common areas, functional layouts)?
- Are outdoor spaces (yard, porch, patio) inviting for family activities or entertaining?

7. Self-Actualization (family growth, legacy, fulfillment)
- Does your home nurture your family's values, traditions, and lifestyle?
- Does it give your children, relatives, or guests an environment to thrive and grow?
- Does your home environment allow you to cultivate deeper friendships and meaningful family connections?
- Does your home feel like the right place to create lasting memories and a sense of legacy?

Now that you have completed the Wheel House Assessment section of Family and Friends and reviewed your answers, before you move on to the next section, shade in your score from 1–10 in the Family and Friends section on the Wheel House Assessment pie chart. Then highlight any significant findings, either good or bad, in the note section for the area of Family and Friends on your Wheel House Assessment worksheet. These findings will be beneficial for you to have as you rearrange areas of your home or discuss your potential relocation or renovation plans with your local agent, designer, or contractor.

Chapter 19

SPIRITUALITY

There is a magic in that little world, home; it is a mystic circle that surrounds comforts and virtues never known beyond its hallowed limits.

—ROBERT SOUTHEY

Coming home to a place of refuge and authenticity will help you become more fully actualized spiritually. A new form of design is trending. Experts say that as humans tap into their innermost, authentic selves in their routines, spiritual home design is having a moment. People are looking at their living spaces in a more holistic, spiritual way.

Creating spaces that connect to your spirit and natural energy goes beyond selecting traditional furniture and color schemes. Thinking beyond just function and aesthetics, the trend is to view the home in light of well-being. Until now, this enlightening thought process has only occurred in the therapist's office, church, synagogue, mosque, or yoga studio. Well-being and balance on a soul level are being incorporated into a style that matches the homeowner's spiritual journey.

To be clear, several ancient philosophies have focused on the soul-home connection—Ayurveda and Feng Shui, for example. In Feng Shui, the Chinese way of life, the fundamental ancient Chinese principles revolve around how your environment produces positive outcomes in your life. You can balance your emotions and energy by using the energies of fire, earth, metal, and wood in your home.

In Ayurveda, a more individualistic approach allows for a balance tailored to an individual's specific body energy. The three types of energy are Vata, the energy of movement; Pitta, the energy of digestion; and Kapha, the energy of the structure. You have a dominant, a secondary, and a least-prominent energy in your body. Like Feng Shui, health issues and suffering are believed to arise when the body and soul are out of balance. The environment is manipulated to keep your body and soul in balance.

By considering your personality, physical makeup, and health, you can use your home environment to address potential imbalances and create a space for refueling and reenergizing so you can come back into the world as your best self. Utilizing different rooms in your home to address specific needs or provide lifestyle elements for everyone is a key aspect of spiritual and soul fulfillment within the Wheel House Assessment.

It starts again with knowing who you are—your body type, personality, and current health level. By understanding the environments that fuel and deplete you, you can create spaces in your home to tap into your spiritual side and enhance your energy and mental health.

Creating space in your home that reflects your and your family's deepest values and dreams takes creativity, understanding, and intuitive guidance. Your home should reflect all your aspirations, beliefs, and what you consider essential in life. The decor and function of each room should reflect what fills up you and your family. Your home should be a sanctuary for your soul and the foundation for achieving your dreams and those of the people around you.

Clarity Farm was where I learned to be still. The natural setting was nothing short of sacred. Every morning I stepped outside and felt closer to God than I ever had sitting in a pew. The rolling hills, the way sunlight filtered through the trees, and the symphony of geese as they flew past the house and through the valley every morning and every night were all His handiwork, and I was living right in the middle of it. I had space to breathe, reflect, and pray without interruption. In those quiet moments, I could hear myself think. I could hear God speak.

For that alone, I'd give Clarity Farm a 10 out of 10 for Spirituality. But here's what kept it from being a 10. While the farm brought me closer to God in solitude, it pulled me farther from the community that helped me practice my faith with others—and that mattered more than I initially realized.

Our church was a half-hour drive away. That might not sound like much, but when you have a family to wrangle, animals to tend, and a property that demands constant attention, those thirty minutes become a barrier. Midweek Bible studies? Sunday evening services? Volunteer opportunities? They all required advanced planning and a willingness to spend more time in the car than at the event itself. We missed out on so much of the church life that had once been such a vibrant part of our routine.

I loved hosting church playgroups at our home. Moms would bring their kids out to the country, and the children would run wild—feeding horses, exploring the lake, playing in wide-open spaces they didn't have at home. It was joyful and life-giving. But for most families, getting to Clarity Farm meant a thirty- to sixty-minute drive. What should have been a simple Tuesday morning playdate became a half-day expedition. Over time, fewer people came. And while I understood, it stung.

Then I broke my back.

The yoga studio that became my sanctuary during recovery—the place I learned to heal, to get stronger, to find myself again—was forty minutes away. On days when my body ached and my spirit felt fragile, that drive felt insurmountable. But I went anyway because I needed it. That mat, that practice, and that community of people who moved and breathed and struggled alongside me were essential to my healing.

And that's the tension I lived with at Clarity Farm. The peace was profound. The connection to nature was soul-nourishing. But the distance from my church, from my yoga studio, and from the people who helped me practice my faith and tend to my spirit was too far.

Spirituality isn't just about quiet reflection, as beautiful as that is. It's also about community. It's about showing up, being seen, and walking alongside others on the same journey. Your home should support both the solitude your soul needs and your ability to connect with the practices and people that keep you grounded.

At Clarity Farm, I had peace. But I was missing the proximity to the places and faces that made my faith and groundedness feel fully alive.

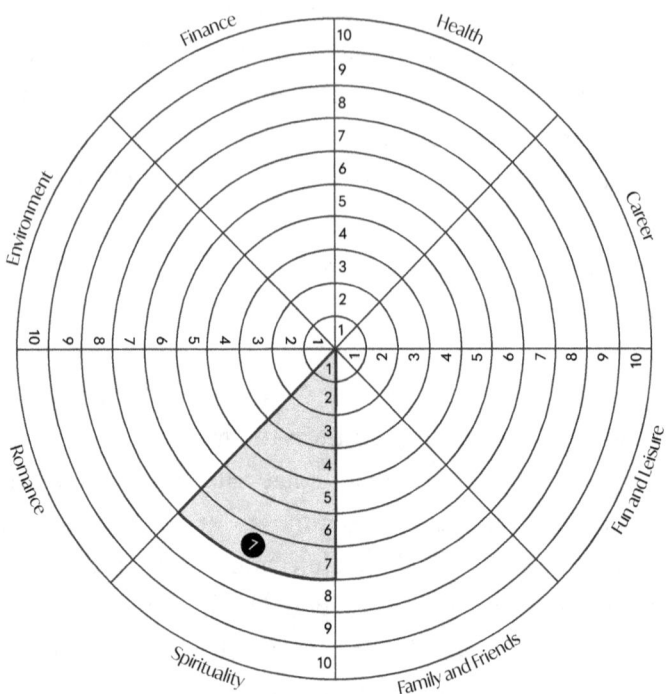

Wheel House Success Story

Rosa's Spirituality Transformation

Before

Rosa had spent most of her adult life as a self-proclaimed workaholic. Her home reflected that pace—efficient but not exactly nurturing. After a series of life changes, she began to question her priorities, realizing that life was too short to rush through. She found solace at a yoga studio in the next town and joined the church next door, and both opened doors to new friendships and a more profound sense of connection. But at home, she felt a disconnect. She often prayed and meditated in her bedroom but longed for a space that truly felt sacred. While her spirit stirred as she tended the church's memorial garden, she yearned for a way to bring that sense of peace and fellowship into her own home.

The Shift

Exploring her Wheel House spirituality questions helped Rosa realize what was missing: Her home wasn't aligned with her evolving values. She needed a setting that nurtured connection to her faith, her community, and her own spirit. Instead of treating spirituality as something that happened *outside* her home, Rosa saw she could bring it closer, creating spaces that invited reflection, prayer, and fellowship right where she lived.

After

Rosa found a home closer to her church and yoga studio, and even within walking distance of a library where she could reserve and check out books for her Bible study. She now hosts gatherings in her garden and on her front porch, serving meals and sharing her famous ripe tomatoes with fellow parishioners. Inside, she carved out a meditation and prayer room complete with a small table for candles and a cozy chair for reading. The space feels blessed, peaceful, and deeply connected to her spirit. Rosa says that her house is no longer just where she lives; it's part of her spiritual journey. Friends who visit often say they feel instantly welcome and loved, which for Rosa is the greatest confirmation that her home is now spiritually aligned.

Now it's time for you to assess your current home versus your ideal home's score in Spirituality on the Wheel House Assessment. Grab your Wheel House Assessment worksheet and write notes regarding your thoughts after considering the following questions and any other scenarios not included here. Remember to write any notes that stand out on the corresponding area for Spirituality on the second page of your worksheet as you read through the Spirituality questions.

Spirituality Questions

1. Physiological Needs (basic comfort for practice and expression)
- Do you have a quiet space in your home for meditation, prayer, or yoga?
- Are there food shops or resources nearby that support your spiritual or dietary practices (e.g., kosher, halal, vegetarian)?
- Is your home's environment physically peaceful and comfortable enough to allow you to relax into spiritual practices?

2. Safety Needs (freedom, security, stability)
- Are there any prejudices, persecutions, or barriers to worship in your community?
- Do you feel emotionally and spiritually safe practicing your beliefs at home or in your community?

- Are there supportive community structures (e.g., freedom of religion laws, safe spaces) that allow you to practice without fear?

3. Love and Belonging (community, connection, shared beliefs)
    - Are there religious services, gatherings, or spiritual communities nearby that align with your faith or practice?
    - Do you feel connected to people of a similar mindset, values, or beliefs in your area?
    - Is there a community where you feel welcome to worship, reflect, or celebrate holidays?
    - Is your home close to the places that matter to your spiritual life (church, synagogue, mosque, yoga center, retreat center)?

4. Esteem Needs (pride, confidence, identity)
    - Does your home reflect and enhance your spiritual expression through symbols, art, or design?
    - Do you feel proud to host or share your spiritual practices (holidays, rituals, or gatherings) in your home?
    - Does your environment allow you to honor your values and beliefs openly?

5. Cognitive Needs (meaning, growth, awareness)
    - Does your home give you space to reflect, read, or study spiritual or philosophical texts?

- Is your environment conducive to learning, self-discovery, and the expansion of spiritual awareness?
- Does your home provide reminders or inspiration that help you stay aligned with your beliefs and values?

6. Aesthetic Needs (beauty, peace, harmony)
   - Does your home feel peaceful, energizing, and balanced in ways that support your spiritual well-being?
   - Do natural elements (light, air, gardens, water features) in or around your home enhance your sense of harmony?
   - Does your home have beauty and symbolism that uplift your spirit?

7. Self-Actualization (purpose, fulfillment, higher meaning)
   - Does your home help you live authentically and express your highest spiritual values?
   - Does it nurture your sense of purpose, meaning, and connection to something greater than yourself?
   - Does your environment inspire spiritual growth, gratitude, and contribution to others?

Now that you have completed the Wheel House Assessment section of Spirituality and reviewed your answers, before you move on to the next section, shade your score from 1–10 in the Spirituality section on the Wheel House Assessment pie chart. Then highlight any significant findings, either good or bad, in the note section for the area of Spirituality on your Wheel House Assessment worksheet.

These findings will be helpful as you rearrange areas of your home or discuss your potential relocation or renovation plans with your local agent, designer, or contractor.

Chapter 20

ROMANCE

*Love is the expansion of two natures in such
fashion that each include the other,
each is enriched by the other.*

—FELIX ADLER

When it comes to supporting romance in your home and life, it is essential to understand the personalities of the two partners involved. What one person enjoys, another might not. The first underlying key to any successful romantic relationship is understanding, and the second is unconditional love. After that, it's about compromise and service to the other.

Fundamentally, whether you are in a new relationship or have been together for thirty years, there must be a willingness to understand each other. Do you know your partner's MBTI or Enneagram? Do you know their love language? What are their pet peeves, their hopes and dreams, their fears, and their life's mission?

After understanding these things about your partner and discussing them with each other, you will feel like you know them, and they in turn will feel seen and understood. This discovery of each other is crucial to the comfort level needed for true spiritual, intellectual, and sexual companionship.

The following tips from Victor Cheung of Feng Shui Nexus invite you to bring more romance into your life with the following intentional love tips for your primary bedroom.

- Get a good, solid headboard. It provides security and stability, and improves your sleep and bedroom play with less sound distraction.
- Freshen up your bedsheets and linens.
- Place your bed properly. Do not place it under a window or in a corner where one person feels trapped or must climb over the other.

- Remove extra pillows and stuffed animals to convey that you only have room for your partner.
- Carefully select your bedroom art. Do not place anything in your bedroom that depicts violence, sorrow, or religion as it provokes emotions that distract you. Instead, use artwork that depicts love and comfort.
- Get rid of the television.
- Get rid of any work papers or tools. Say goodbye to the home office in the primary bedroom.
- Bedside furniture should be symmetrical. There should be no better side of the bed.
- Declutter. Clutter is a stress-producer.
- Remove photographs of friends and family from the bedroom. This is your intimate space. These photos in your bedroom can make you feel like people are looking at you.
- Increase the yin energy of the bedroom by incorporating light dimmers, soft music, flowing fabrics, and relaxing colors.[30]

While the primary bedroom is romance central in your home, there are other ways to enhance your romantic relationship throughout your home. The primary bathroom—as well as other features in the home such as an intimate dining area, a cozy nook for two to read or watch TV together, or separate areas for each partner to refuel and transition to time for intimacy—can all be considered as you consciously turn up the heat on romance in your home.

Clarity Farm had all the ingredients for romance—on paper anyway. Privacy? We had it in spades. Peace and quiet? More than we knew what to do with. Tranquility? The kind you see in movies with sunsets so brilliant right from the front porch and nights so still you could hear your own heartbeat except in the summer. Every bug, croaking frog, and pack of coyotes would interrupt the peace.

It should have been the perfect setting for romance. And sometimes it was. There's something undeniably intimate about being tucked away from the world, just the two of you, surrounded by beauty and nature sounds. But here's what the brochure doesn't tell you about rural romance: It requires a lot of work.

Want a romantic dinner out? First, you have to find a babysitter willing to make the trek to your remote location and willing to drive home on the dark gravel road. Then you have to drive twenty minutes (minimum) to the closest restaurant. By the time you get there, you're exhausted from coordinating logistics, and the spontaneity that makes date nights magical has evaporated.

Want a romantic dinner at home? Great! Now you're the chef, the server, and the cleanup crew. And if you've spent the day tending to animals, mowing acres of land, or fixing whatever broke that week (because something always broke), the last thing you feel like doing is setting the mood over a stove, no matter how lovely your kitchen is.

And even when we did carve out time together, there was another challenge: My former spouse and I ran a successful family business together. We were business partners as much as life partners, which meant our conversations—even the ones that should have been romantic—had a way of drifting back to work, invoices, client issues, and scheduling conflicts. It's hard to keep the spark alive when you're discussing payroll over candlelight.

The truth is that Clarity Farm gave us too much privacy and not enough opportunity. Romance thrives on variety—on getting dressed up and going somewhere new, on spontaneous adventures, on moments that don't require an hour of prep work and a detailed exit strategy. At the farm, every romantic gesture became a production. And while I'm all for effort, romance shouldn't feel like a second job when you're already exhausted.

If I'm being honest, I'd score Romance at Clarity Farm a 5 out of 10. When romance requires that much effort just to happen—or when work bleeds into every conversation—it often doesn't happen at all.

Your home should support your relationship, not make it harder to nurture. It should offer privacy when you need it, yes, but also proximity to the experiences that keep your connection alive. While sunsets are beautiful, they can't replace the spark that comes from dancing in a crowded restaurant, holding hands on a city street, or simply having the freedom to go out without needing a battle plan.

Today, the cottage my husband Rocky and I share is a completely different story—but that's a tale for another chapter.

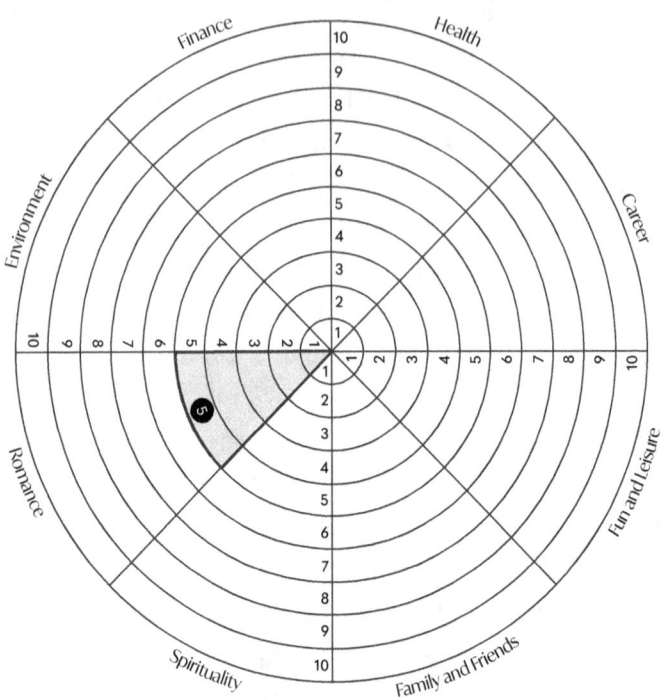

Wheel House Success Story

Lila's Romance Transformation

Before

Lila, recently divorced, felt trapped in her swanky section of the city. Everyone knew about her breakup, and to make matters worse, her ex was parading his new girlfriend around like a float in the Thanksgiving Day parade. The thought of bumping into them at the grocery store was enough to keep Lila home in sweatpants. To top it off, nearly everyone in her community was married with kids, and the single crowd that *did* exist seemed like a poor fit. Lila, a self-proclaimed outdoorsy girl, was living in a sea of men in suits. The local dating scene made her feel like she needed stilettos and heavy makeup just to be considered "in the game," and that simply wasn't her.

The Shift

When Lila began answering her Wheel House Romance questions, it became clear that her environment was completely misaligned with who she was and what she wanted. She wasn't the problem; her zip code was. Once she gave herself permission to consider *anywhere* as home, a whole new world of possibilities opened. Together, we researched cities with better dating demographics, vibrant single communities, and, most importantly, opportunities for outdoor adventure.

After

After exploratory trips to San Diego, Austin, and Denver, Lila's heart landed firmly in the Rockies. In Denver she found not only an outdoorsy, adventurous crowd but also a ratio that worked more in her favor. With a trusted real estate agent (who quickly became a friend), Lila found a home base that reflected her lifestyle. Now she spends weekends hiking and skiing instead of dodging awkward run-ins at the local grocery store. Best of all, she's meeting suitors who share her love of the outdoors, and her confidence has returned. Lila laughs that she traded her high heels for hiking boots, and for once she's not tripping over either.

Now it's time for you to assess your current home versus your ideal home's score in Romance on the Wheel House Assessment. Grab your Wheel House Assessment worksheet and write notes regarding your thoughts after considering the following questions and any other scenarios relevant to you in the area of Romance. Remember to write any notes that stand out in the corresponding area for Romance on the second page of your worksheet as you read through the Romance questions.

Romance Questions

1. Physiological Needs (comfort, sensory experience)
- Is your bed and bedding comfortable?
- Is your bedroom set up for romance and intimacy (lighting, ambiance, cleanliness)?
- Does your home have features that invite relaxation (bathtub, cozy nooks)?
- Do noises, drafts, smells, or temperature affect intimacy?

2. Safety Needs (emotional and physical security)
- Is your home private, safe, and quiet enough for intimacy?
- Are both you and your partner comfortable living here?
- Do you feel emotionally safe expressing affection in your home?
- Are you proud to bring a date or partner home (clean, uncluttered, in good repair)?

3. Love and Belonging (connection, companionship, affection)
   - Does your home provide spaces for togetherness as well as time alone?
   - Are there cozy, intimate areas beyond the bedroom (living room, porch, etc.)?
   - Does your private space (bedroom, bathroom, closet) feel welcoming and attractive—even for a future partner if you're dating?
   - Do you have spaces for shared rituals (morning coffee, meals, or evening wind-down)?
   - Is there a place to enjoy hobbies, activities, or interests with your partner?

4. Esteem Needs (pride, confidence, fairness, respect)
   - Does your home reflect both of your personalities fairly?
   - Is your bedroom and bedside area set up for equal comfort?
   - Are personal spaces balanced, not dominated by one partner's needs or tastes?
   - Are you proud of your home as a space for romance and connection?

5. Cognitive Needs (awareness, reflection, shared growth)
   - Do you live in a town or community with opportunities to meet new people if desired?

- Does your home environment support your current stage (single, dating, married, transitioning)?
- Does your home provide space for meaningful conversations and shared growth?
- Does your environment encourage exploration together (a reading nook, a hobby space, a media area)?

6. Aesthetic Needs (beauty, romance, harmony)
- Does your bedroom feel romantic or cluttered with distractions?
- Is it easy to set a romantic mood in your home (lighting, music, ambiance)?
- Do you intentionally use decor, art, or colors that feel soothing and romantic?
- Are there areas designed for special moments (date nights, cozy movie nights)?

7. Self-Actualization (romance as fulfillment, highest expression of love)
- Does your home environment encourage deeper intimacy and authentic connection?
- Does your space nurture both passion and long-term companionship?
- Does your romantic environment reflect the love life you aspire to create?
- Does your home support joy, self-expression, and growth through your relationships?

Now that you have completed the Wheel House Assessment section of Romance and reviewed your answers, before you move on to the next section, shade in your score from 1–10 in the Romance section on the Wheel House Assessment pie chart. Then highlight any significant findings, either good or bad, in the note section for the area of Romance on your Wheel House Assessment worksheet. These findings will be helpful as you rearrange areas of your home or discuss your potential relocation or renovation plans with your local agent, designer, or contractor.

Chapter 21

ENVIRONMENT

If your environment is not to your liking, change it!

—NAPOLEON HILL

The environment we live in affects many aspects of our lives: our well-being, opinions, social interactions, thinking, and mood. Some examples of environmental factors that influence our lives are noise, air and water pollution, availability of natural resources, access to health care, weather, educational opportunities, food sources, cultural norms, traffic patterns, political climate, economic opportunities, crime rates, and the spirit of the community.

Along with these outside-the-home environmental attributes, the inside of your home plays a large part in your emotional and physical well-being. According to Lena Abalone in the article "How Your Environment Affects Your Emotions," "People tend to have higher levels of well-being when they live in attractive, warm, and cozy properties. Their homes recharge their batteries, so to speak, enabling them to take on the world's challenges with more confidence. Well-being tends to decline when properties are dilapidated, dirty, or affected by dampness."[31]

Environmental factors that affect you are paramount to living a stable, familiar, safe life—the lowest attributes on Maslow's Hierarchy of Needs. In a November 2024 article in the *Journal of Environmental Psychology*, authors Daniel Stokols and Ruth Barankevich stated, "Among the diverse settings that comprise the ecology of individuals' daily experiences—from their dwellings, classrooms and workplaces to their healthcare settings, neighborhood and community spaces—scholars have long regarded places of residence as uniquely important in people's lives and closely tied to their emotional and physical well-being."[32]

Clare Cooper described the house as a *symbol of the self* and observed that design and decoration of domestic spaces not only mirror but also reinforce inhabitants' feelings about themselves and their unique personal identities."[33]

The article by Stokols and Barankevich goes on to say that a homeowner's security is mainly seen through the lens of "the nearby environment, including one's capacity to afford high quality housing, defensible space design of the dwelling, and the absence of nearby threats such as fire and flood hazards, seismic risks, and undesirable land uses like oil drilling sites, landfills, and congested roadways."[34] In addition to the environmental characteristics, we must also consider weather, noise pollution, sign pollution, crime, demographics, and many other factors that affect the environment we live in.

Clarity Farm was a slice of heaven. There's no other way to describe it. The fresh air was so clean it revived you. Views stretched across the Little River Valley in layers of green and gold, changing with the seasons like a living painting. We grew organic vegetables that tasted the way food is supposed to, full of flavor and nourishing. A cutting garden gave us endless perennials for the dinner table. We had a swimming pool that sparkled under the Georgia sun, a barn and entertaining pavilion built for gathering, and beautiful horses grazing behind four-board fencing that created a scene that looked like it belonged on the cover of *Southern Living*.

The property wasn't just beautiful; it was soul-restoring. It was the kind of place where you could step outside at dawn and feel the weight of the world lift off your shoulders.

I've traveled. I've seen stunning homes and breathtaking landscapes. But Clarity Farm remains the most beautiful place I've ever laid eyes on. And that's why, despite everything—the remoteness, the logistical challenges, all the ways it didn't align with other areas of my life—I still score Environment at Clarity Farm a 10 out of 10.

Some things transcend practicality. Some places touch something deeper than convenience or proximity. Clarity Farm fed my soul in ways I didn't even know I needed. It reminded me daily that I was part of something bigger: God's creation in all its glory. It gave me space to breathe, to heal, and to see beauty in a world that often feels too loud and too fast.

Words can't fully capture what it felt like to live there. You had to experience it—the way the morning mist hung over the valley, the way the horses frollicked across the pasture, and the way the sunset turned the sky into a masterpiece every evening.

Yes, the remoteness created problems in other areas of my life. Yes, it made romance harder, community harder, and career logistics more complicated. But when it came to the environment—the physical beauty, the air I breathed, the land I walked on—Clarity Farm was perfection.

Your environment matters more than most people realize. It shapes your mood, your energy, and your sense of well-being. And while a beautiful environment alone can't fix misalignment in other areas of your life, it can sustain you in ways that are hard to quantify.

Clarity Farm sustained me. It filled my cup. It showed me what's possible when you surround yourself with natural beauty and create space for peace.

And even though I've moved on and know it wasn't the right fit for every area of my Wheel House, I'll never forget what it gave me.

Some places leave a mark on your soul. Clarity Farm left a 10 out of 10 for beauty.

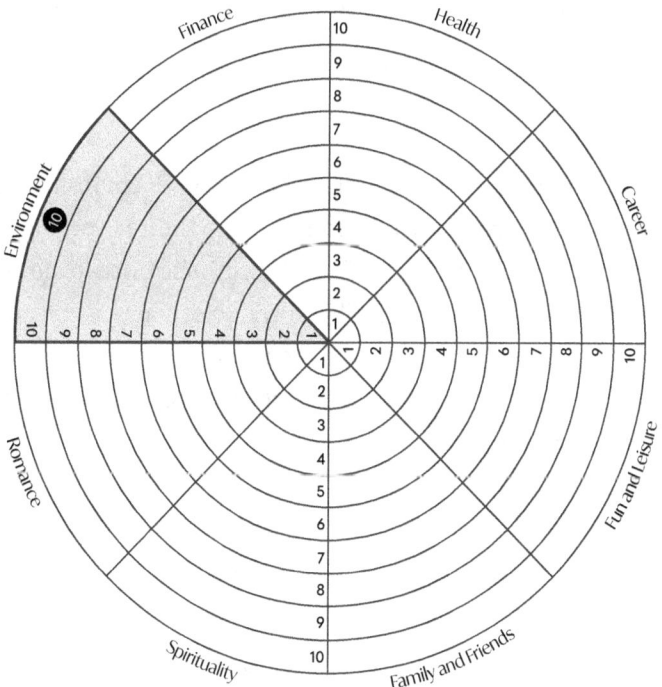

Wheel House Success Story
Sandra's Environment Transformation

Before
Sandra loved her charming bungalow—or at least she *used to*. Over the years, her once-cozy neighborhood had changed. Traffic clogged the streets at all hours, the air carried a permanent haze from nearby industry, and the barking dogs and late-night parties from next door made peaceful sleep a fantasy. She tried to ignore it, convincing herself it was "just city life," but the truth was her environment was eroding her energy. Even her allergies had gotten worse, and she found herself spending more weekends indoors with the windows shut tight.

The Shift
When Sandra answered her Wheel House environment questions, she realized her home wasn't the real problem; it was where the home was. The city vibe she once loved no longer matched her needs. She craved clean air, safety, and a sense of peace. For Sandra, the environment wasn't about having a prettier house; it was about creating a backdrop for healthier living.

After
Sandra sold her bungalow and moved to a newer home on the edge of town near hiking trails and a friendly, quieter community. Instead of the constant buzz of traffic, she now hears birds in the morning. Her allergies have improved

with better air quality, and the neighbors are more likely to invite her for coffee than keep her up past midnight. She's discovered that peace and productivity are easier to find when your environment supports you. Sandra jokes that the loudest thing in her yard is her wind chimes.

It's time now for you to assess your current home versus your ideal home's score in Environment on the Wheel House Assessment. Grab your Wheel House Assessment worksheet and write notes regarding your thoughts on your current and your ideal environment after considering the following questions and any other scenarios relevant to you that aren't covered here. Remember to write any notes that stand out on the corresponding area for Environment on the second page of your worksheet as you read through the Environment questions.

Environment Questions

1. Physiological Needs (basic livability, comfort, nature access)
- Does the climate in your area feel comfortable and supportive of your health and lifestyle?
- Do you get enough natural light in your home, or does it feel dreary?
- Are there issues with water, air, or noise pollution that affect your well-being?
- Are seasonal allergies, insects, or wildlife a problem in your area?

- Does the natural environment (mountains, beach, city, small town, etc.) align with your lifestyle needs?

2. Safety Needs (security, stability, protection)
- Is your neighborhood safe from crime?
- Is the area prone to flooding, climate change risks, or severe weather issues?
- How is the traffic, parking, and general ease of access to your community?
- Are your neighbors respectful of boundaries (not noisy, invasive, or threatening)?
- Does your HOA or local governance create restrictions or rules that impact your lifestyle positively or negatively?
- Is eminent domain, new construction, or utility expansion (power lines, sewer, etc.) a concern?

3. Love and Belonging (community, connection, relationships)
- Are your neighbors welcoming and friendly, and do you feel connected in your community?
- Do you feel your community has people in your stage of life (young families, retirees, LGBTQ+ inclusivity, etc.)?
- Do you have supportive social spaces nearby (churches, gyms, clubs, social groups)?
- Does your community have a vibe or persona that feels like "you" (artsy, suburban, small-town, energetic city, etc.)?

- Do you have roommates or cohabitants who support—or hinder—your comfort and peace?

4. Esteem Needs (pride, fit, alignment with personal identity)
- Does the style and architecture of your home reflect your personality (traditional, modern, eclectic, etc.)?
- Does the decor and artwork inside your home express your true self?
- Is your neighborhood's socioeconomic status (affluent, middle-class, modest) aligned with how you see yourself?
- Do you feel proud to invite people into your home and community?
- Are your home's space and storage appropriate (not too little, not overwhelming clutter)?

5. Cognitive Needs (awareness, exploration, growth)
- Is your home conveniently located near the places that matter (work, airport, schools, daycare, health care)?
- Is your home close to hobbies and activities you enjoy (golf, boating, skiing, restaurants, arts)?
- Do you understand how local government policies, taxes, and zoning affect your home environment?
- Are you aware of long-term environmental concerns that affect your area (erosion, infrastructure changes, eminent domain)?

6. Aesthetic Needs (beauty, harmony, design, inspiration)
   - What views does your home offer (mountains, city skyline, water, trees)?
   - Does your environment feel balanced, attractive, and inspiring to you?
   - Does the floor plan of your home suit your lifestyle (open vs. closed concept)?
   - Does the community or surrounding environment add beauty (walkable streets, gardens, architecture)?

7. Self-Actualization (purpose, fulfillment, alignment with vision)
   - Does your environment support the lifestyle you aspire to (freedom, adventure, tranquility, creativity)?
   - Does your home's location and community allow you to live authentically, aligned with your values?
   - Does your home's environment inspire you to grow, contribute, or express your highest potential?
   - Do you feel your home's environment is a launching pad for the next chapter of your life?

Now that you have completed the Wheel House Assessment section of Environment and reviewed your answers, before you move on to the next section, shade in your score from 1–10 in the Environment section on the Wheel House Assessment pie chart. Then highlight any significant findings, either good or bad, in the note section for the area of Environment on your Wheel House Assessment worksheet. These findings will be helpful as you rearrange areas of your home or discuss your potential relocation or renovation plans with your local agent, designer, or contractor.

Chapter 22

FINANCE

Financial freedom is available to those who learn about it and work for it.

—ROBERT KIYOSAKI

In the area of finance, there are many aspects of your home you need to consider. The first step is to assess your financial resources and determine if you can afford the home you own while also saving for retirement, vacations, and the lifestyle you desire.

Conversely, are you underhoused? If your current house lacks features that match your desired lifestyle, do you have the income, liquid assets, and future funds to afford and maintain a larger or more expensive home?

After consulting with a financial advisor and a lender (if appropriate) to review your net worth and financial qualifications, you can assess the financial resources available for your home. Some of the considerations that come into play in this analysis are inheritance money, debt, passive income, upcoming financial obligations (e.g., college, weddings), planning for illnesses or disabilities, elder or childcare, and retirement planning. Your financial advisors will be instrumental in preparing this analysis.

Below are some examples of a home that does not fit your financial needs and capabilities:

- Too big for your current lifestyle
- Too many maintenance costs or high HOA fees
- Property taxes that are too high
- Impending decrease in the value of your home
- Receiving an inheritance that affords you more of your "dream home"
- Does not have enough room for an office, home gym, entertainment, hobby, storage, or other space you may need to outsource

- Repairs or renovations needed
- An investment property that is not grossing enough income to cover carrying costs
- A vacation home you've lost interest in and don't visit often
- A primary home you often take vacations to get away from
- Insurance costs, including flood or disaster risk
- High equity in your home, and you need those funds
- "In the red" in your current monthly budget

While purchasing a home is a significant first step to building personal wealth, financial planning is just beginning. Keep the momentum going to make a firm economic foundation for your future.

The first step to understanding your financial status and planning is to create a net worth statement and a monthly budget that summarizes your income and expenses. These two financial documents are a snapshot of your financial health and should be revised and reviewed at least annually.

From these documents, you can move on to financial and retirement planning with the help of your advisors. According to the U.S. Census Bureau, in 2022, about half of Americans ages fifty-five to sixty-six had no retirement savings, with women showing far less savings than men.[35] You don't want to retire broke. Being frugal doesn't have to mean you're not living your best life. It just means you must prioritize and better allocate your spending to take advantage of full and early retirement.

Because your home is the most significant living expense—35 percent of the average American's take-home pay after taxes—it is wise to evaluate if your home is regularly meeting both your lifestyle and financial needs. The Wheel House process will help you live purposefully and with the security that your financial future is safe in a home that best suits you.

Clarity Farm wasn't just a home—it was an investment, a passion project, and proof that sweat equity pays off. We developed that land from scratch. What started as unusable acreage became rolling pastures, a meticulously designed home, and a property that turned heads. Using our residential construction and design skills, we transformed the land with careful grading and drainage, and then worked alongside an architect and general contractor to bring our vision to life. We were hands-on in every phase, making decisions that balanced beauty with smart building practices.

And it paid off—big time.

By the time we finished, the value of the home far exceeded the money we'd put into it. As we lived at Clarity Farm, the property continued to climb in value. Every improvement we made and every thoughtful detail we added contributed to its worth. We weren't just living there; we were building equity with every passing year.

Our small family business was thriving and profitable, which meant we could more than afford the home, the acreage, the maintenance, the animals, and the generous lifestyle Clarity Farm provided. We weren't stretched thin or stressed about money. We had margin—the kind of financial breathing room that let us enjoy what we'd built without constantly worrying about the cost.

The financials worked beautifully in other ways too. Taxes were low compared to what we would have paid in a more developed area. There was no HOA fee eating into our budget every month. And because we'd built the home with high-efficiency windows, appliances, and materials, our utilities stayed surprisingly low despite the size of the property. Every choice we made during construction paid dividends in ongoing savings.

Financially, Clarity Farm was a home run. We built wealth. We created something of lasting value—not just in dollars but in what it represented: our skills, our vision, our ability to turn potential into something extraordinary.

For Finance, I score Clarity Farm a 10 out of 10.

It proved that when you invest wisely, build thoughtfully, and align your resources with your vision, your home can be one of the smartest financial decisions you ever make. Clarity Farm became more valuable over time while giving us a lifestyle most people only dream about.

That's the power of a home that works for you financially, not against you.

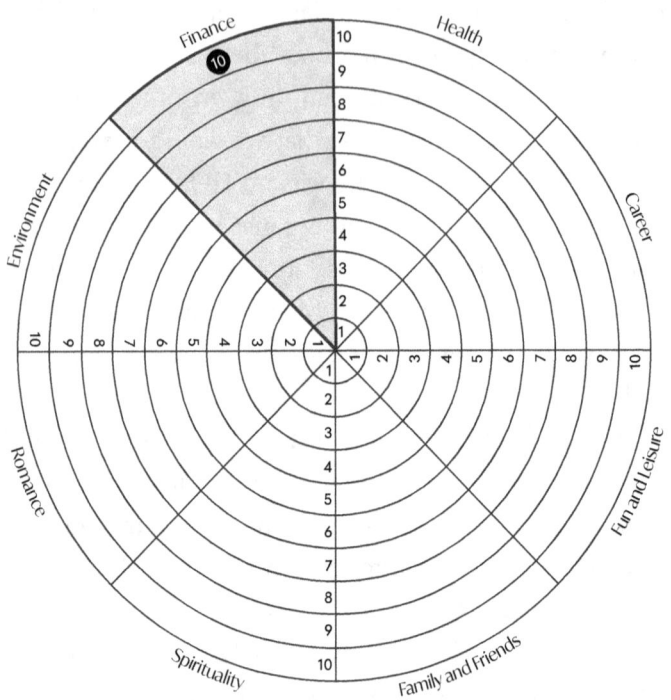

Wheel House Success Story

Jill and Joe's Finance Transformation

Before

Jill and Joe, nearly empty nesters and just a decade away from retirement, had done a lot right—steady saving, careful planning, and keeping only a small mortgage. But when they unexpectedly inherited a million dollars from a relative, their financial picture suddenly looked very different. Alongside the excitement came anxiety. They had always dreamed of owning a place by the beach, but the thought of making a big move so close to retirement brought worry. What if they ended up with an ocean view but no money to buy groceries?

The Shift

Going through their Wheel House finance questions, Jill and Joe realized they didn't have to choose between their dream and their security; they could have both with the right strategy. Instead of clinging to their oversized family home in the city (and its mortgage), they could reframe their inheritance as an opportunity to diversify their lifestyle and assets.

After

With a referral to a trusted real estate agent in their favorite coastal town, Jill and Joe sold their big house in the city and bought a charming, smaller, lock-and-leave home with no mortgage. They then used part of their inheritance to purchase a cozy cottage near the beach that doubles as a short-term rental. The cottage pays for itself most of the year while Jill and Joe get to sneak away for long weekends and plan for extended stays when retirement comes.

Both properties are in rising-value areas, which gives them peace of mind that their assets will grow along with their joy. Jill jokes that she and Joe are "officially landlords with flip-flops," while Joe is just happy he won't be mowing two big lawns in retirement.

Now it's time for you to assess your current home versus your ideal home's score in Finance on the Wheel House Assessment. Grab your Wheel House Assessment worksheet and write notes regarding your thoughts after considering the following questions and any other scenarios that might be relevant. Remember to write any notes that stand out on the corresponding area for Finance on the second page of your worksheet as you read through the Finance questions.

Finance Questions

1. Physiological Needs (basic survival: affordability of shelter and essentials)
   - Can you afford your monthly home payments? Conversely, can you afford a bigger or newer home with the features you desire?
   - Can you afford your utilities, maintenance costs, and house payment?
   - Do you have sufficient funds to cover immediate household essentials (repairs, groceries, gas, etc.)?

2. Safety Needs (financial stability, security, risk management)
   - Do you own your home, or is it financed? Will your interest rates, taxes, or HOA fees be increasing?
   - Are you building equity in your home? What is your interest rate? How far along are you with your payments?
   - Will you be incurring any additional family expenses soon (college, medical costs, weddings)?
   - Do you have an emergency fund for unexpected home repairs or life changes?
   - Do you have proper insurance coverage (home-owner's, flood, life, disability) to protect your assets?

- Is your mortgage and debt load at a manageable level for long-term stability?

3. Love and Belonging (family, connection, community security)
   - Will you be receiving any inheritances soon?
   - Are you supporting or cofinancing a home with family (parents, adult children, etc.)?
   - Do your financial resources allow you to host, support, or provide for your loved ones comfortably in your home?

4. Esteem Needs (success, recognition, status through financial progress)
   - How much has your home value increased since you bought it?
   - Are the home values in your area increasing or decreasing?
   - What improvements have you made to your home? What improvements would you like to make?
   - Does your home investment make you feel proud and accomplished?
   - Does your financial situation allow you to participate in charitable giving or community contributions?

5. Cognitive Needs (knowledge, learning, exploration)
   - Are you looking for passive income or rental income opportunities?

- Are you educating yourself on real estate, investing, or tax strategies to optimize your wealth?
- Do you understand the long-term financial implications of your home (equity growth, taxes, estate planning)?

6. Aesthetic Needs (harmony, balance, appreciation of financial beauty)
   - What improvements would you like to make to your home that would bring beauty, harmony, or balance?
   - Do your financial choices allow you to create a home that feels elegant and aligned with your values (not just functional)?

7. Self-Actualization (financial freedom, alignment with life purpose)
   - Does your financial approach to your home allow you to live in alignment with your dreams and highest potential?
   - Do you feel financially free enough to make bold choices (downsizing, upgrading, relocating) that align with your life's vision?
   - Does your home's financial position give you the freedom to pursue your passions, philanthropy, or legacy goals?

Now that you have completed the Wheel House Assessment section of Finance and reviewed your answers, before you move on to the next section, shade in your score from 1–10 in the Finance section on the Wheel

House Assessment pie chart. Then highlight any significant findings, either good or bad, in the note section for the area of Finance on your Wheel House Assessment worksheet. These findings will be beneficial for you to have as you rearrange areas of your home or discuss your potential relocation or renovation plans with your local agent, designer, or contractor.

The Finance Assessment was the last of the eight lifestyle areas of the Wheel House Assessment. It is now time to examine the entire Wheel House Assessment pie chart results as a whole to help you get closer to living in your Wheel House.

Part 5
WHEEL HOUSE ASSESSMENT OUTCOMES

Chapter 23

INTERPRETING YOUR WHEEL HOUSE SCORE

As you review the scores of your Wheel House Assessment, remember that the goal is to make the shape of the colored sections of the wheel as close to a fully inflated wheel as possible rather than a flat tire. The objective is a score of 8–10 in each area.

Of course, we all know that nothing is perfect. No home, job, lifestyle, partner, community, town, or country is ever going to be without flaws. Compromise is inevitable. But your goal is to pick wisely and cultivate the aspects that will collectively bring you the most joy and comfort possible.

As you review the scores and notes from each area of the Wheel House Assessment, note any areas where you scored below 3. Depending on how important you consider this area, it may be a deal-breaker for your current home. Misaligned elements in this area may make it impossible for you to remain in your current home.

Sometimes there is no clear deal-breaker for your current home. If many elements of the Wheel House Assessment scored somewhere between 4 and 7, your wheel might look like a deflating tire. It will get you there, but the road will be bumpy. Take the time to review your notes across all areas to determine what fixing the misalignments might look like. Do the areas of concern point more toward a significant renovation or a move? Or are the concerns minor enough that you can stay and rearrange some rooms and make slight adjustments to correct the flow and function of a space?

If you have a robust, inflated tire shape because of the Wheel House Assessment, congratulations! You are probably living in your Wheel House. A few tweaks here and there, a minor renovation, or moving some furniture around, and you have made it even better. I suggest reexamining your foundation—the 4Ms—to maximize your potential and positive influence on the world. Genuinely living in your Wheel House will bring you and others more joy.

Looking back at my Wheel House Assessment during those Clarity Farm days, my scores told a story I wasn't ready to hear. Health scored a dismal 1. I was barely surviving, let alone thriving. Career limped in at a 2, reflecting just how lost and unfulfilled I felt professionally. Family and Friends registered a 4, and Fun and Leisure matched it at another 4—both areas languishing in mediocrity when they should have been bringing me joy. Romance sat at 5, Spirituality at 7, and both Environment and Finance came in at a respectable 10.

But here's what mattered: When I now plot those numbers on my wheel, I don't see the smooth, balanced circle of a life rolling forward with momentum. I see a flat tire. The most fundamental areas—health, career, family and friends, fun and leisure—were deflated and dragging, while other areas tried to compensate.

I see now what I felt then. You can't build a life on 10s in Environment and Finance when your health is failing and your career feels like a slow death. A wheel that is lopsided doesn't roll; it lurches and wobbles and eventually stops moving altogether. This visual—the honest, unflinching image of my flat tire—represents the wake-up call I needed to understand that transformation wasn't optional; it was survival.

What felt like a choice between living fully or a slow death at the time seemed unfathomable to many looking at my beautiful home. While everything seemed perfect from the outside, I felt stuck, scared, frustrated, and unhappy.

The scored Wheel House Assessment for Clarity Farm is represented below. Over two decades later, I now have the terminology, the tools, the structure, and the visual representation of the changes I needed to make in order to fully live in my Wheel House. And now I also know how to help other people live in their Wheel House.

Wheel House Assessment

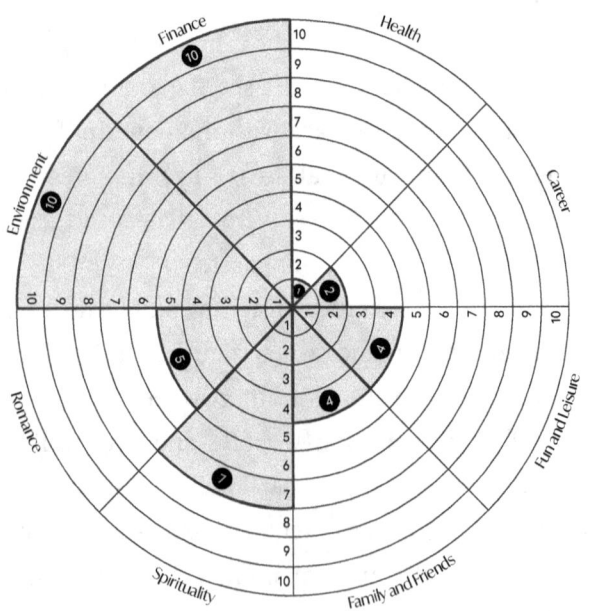

Chapter 24

STAY, GO, OR RENO?

Some people look for a beautiful place, others make a place beautiful.

—HAZRAT INAYAT KHAN

So you have your Wheel House Assessment in hand. You've colored each piece of the wheel and connected the top of the spokes to get your wheel shape. You've examined the notes on each area of the wheel to determine any deal-breakers for your current home, areas where the home excels, and areas in between. Now it's time to decide if you stay, go, or reno.

Is there a clear answer for your next step and direction? Knowing there is rarely a perfect outcome, let's talk through each scenario.

Stay

Your home is nearly perfect. It fits your personality, the expression of your true self, and aligns with almost every area of your ideal lifestyle. I'm thrilled to say that you are likely prioritizing self-esteem, aesthetics, and self-actualization in your self-expression as outlined in Maslow's Hierarchy of Needs. Congratulations!

If you have any notes from the Wheel House Assessment that inspire you to tweak a few things in your home, take action to create even more joy, alignment, and comfort in your home. Consider consulting with a design professional and a real estate agent to get the most bang for your buck. And they can guide you to balance your enjoyment with the most desirable and profitable improvements for your eventual resale.

I want to mention another reason to stay: timing. It might be that you eventually want to move, but the timing isn't right. For example, you live in an excellent public school district, and your youngest child has two more years until graduation. You know you eventually want to move, but you want to stay for now.

The Wheel House Assessment is meant to be taken every time you are experiencing or anticipating a life change. Many homeowners consult their agent to discuss an impending move and make any improvements in anticipation. That way they can get advice on which improvements are most important—bathroom remodel, new roof—before an upcoming sale. That gives you plenty of time to invest and a budget to follow in anticipation of the forthcoming move, all while enjoying the improvements *and* the return on the investment when it comes time to sell.

Go

Your Assessment reveals one or more areas that force a move. You've probably scored the area under a 4. For example, a moldy basement, flooding issues, an unsafe neighborhood, or a lack of adequate space in your home are undeniably misaligned with your health, happiness, and well-being. These are examples of physiological and safety needs not being met. Your Assessment shows that you are not living in your Wheel House.

Another scenario that might compel a move is if many areas of your Wheel House Assessment score below 7. The wheel is not necessarily flat in one area, but it is a tiny wheel. It's just not meeting your full Wheel House potential. For example, there is no room for a pool (Entertainment), there is not enough space to entertain (Family and Friends), your work is too far away (Career), there is no gym nearby (Health), the property taxes are high (Finance), and so on.

You are not miserable in your home, but you know it is lacking in several areas. It's just okay, and you have the means to make a change. It's time to move. Gather your Assessment results and notes, and then call your real estate agent. If you own your current home, it's time to prepare it for sale and look for a new home.

If you are moving out of your area, your local real estate agent can connect you with a reliable agent in your prospective area. Using your Wheel House Assessment findings, your agent(s) will be better equipped to help you meet your goals.

If you do not have an expert local agent and need assistance finding one who is client-focused and familiar with the Wheel House process, please reach out to me at LifestyleFoundations.com.

Reno

If you are finding that the bones, location, and general characteristics of your home are aligning with your goals and preferences, you might consider a renovation, a rearrangement of furniture, or a design tweak to meet your Wheel House goals. A renovation can improve your home's appearance, usability, and resale value. Other goals include increasing your home's energy efficiency and comfort, saving money, and receiving tax credits.

Generally, you can use a home decorator to change color schemes, rearrange furniture, or help achieve a desired aesthetic. In contrast, you might use an interior designer to handle structural changes or collaborate with contractors or architects. Interior designers plan the spatial layout of rooms and ensure that the spaces meet safety standards and building codes. A good reminder before you embark on a remodel project is that you, the homeowner, are responsible for all code violations and safety issues as a result of a remodel, primarily if you or the contractor did not obtain the required permits from your local planning and zoning department's jurisdiction.

A word to the wise: More likely than not, any code or safety discrepancies will be discovered during the inspection by the next buyer of the home. And most likely the buyer will ask for those fixes. I've also seen local planning and zoning departments fine the homeowner who did not obtain the required building permits for a remodel. Make sure to check out your local rules and regulations or hire a qualified professional who is familiar with them, and make the arrangements necessary to stay within your local permit and code requirements. You'll thank me later.

Conclusion

THE WHEEL HOUSE HALL OF FAME

*I shall participate, I shall contribute,
and in so doing, I will be the gainer.*

—WALTER ANNENBERG

I hope this book has helped you identify your true self and your ideal living environment. Living in your Wheel House involves achieving alignment, comfort, and joy so you have the time, freedom, resources, and inclination to help other people.

In the Wheel House Method illustration, self-actualization and transcendence are achieved when you progress through the lower needs from physiological through aesthetic. The attic space represents the height of living in your Wheel House. It's similar to how Carl Jung created a tower addition to his home on Seestrasse on the shores of Lake Zurich at the culmination of his life.

Jung's tower wasn't just an addition to his home; it was the physical manifestation of a life's work integrated. He built it as a place for reflection, for diving more deeply into the questions that had consumed him, for creating space to give back the wisdom he'd accumulated. The tower represented his transcendence—his ability to rise above the daily demands and dedicate himself to something larger.

That's what happens when you truly live in your Wheel House. Once your foundation is solid—when your basic needs are met, your relationships are nourishing, your environment supports your authentic self, and your days reflect your values—you naturally begin to look outward. You stop merely surviving or even thriving for yourself alone. You start asking, *How can I serve? What can I contribute? Who needs what I've learned?*

This is the attic space of your life. It's where purpose meets impact. It's where you discover that alignment isn't selfish. It's actually the prerequisite for your most generous self.

I've seen this transformation on my own journey. When I was struggling to figure out who I was or where I belonged, I had little capacity to think beyond my own needs. But as I aligned my work with my mission, my home with my values, and my relationships with my authentic self, something shifted. Suddenly I had the energy, clarity, and desire to create the Wheel House Method—not just for me but for everyone searching for that same alignment.

When you reach your attic—when you've done the work of aligning each area of your life—you'll find yourself with a new kind of freedom, not freedom *from* responsibility but freedom *for* contribution. You'll have time you didn't know existed. You'll have resources—emotional, mental, financial—that aren't completely depleted by the end of each day. And most importantly, you'll have the inclination to share what you've discovered with others still searching.

Maybe you'll mentor someone who is navigating a career transition. Maybe you'll open your home to foster deeper community connections. Maybe you'll create something—art, a business, a movement—that helps others find their own alignment. Whatever form it takes, your transcendence will naturally flow into service.

Jung built his tower. The Annenbergs created Sunnylands, a home so aligned with their values of diplomacy, culture, and connection that it became a gathering place for world leaders and change-makers. These aren't just beautiful spaces; they're testaments to what becomes possible when you live fully in your Wheel House.

So here's my invitation to you: Don't just read this book and set it aside. Use it. Return to the eight areas. Assess honestly where you are. Make the changes, however small, that move you toward alignment. Build your foundation and then your walls, and then climb to your attic because the world needs what you have to offer. But only living fully as yourself can give it. Your Wheel House is waiting. And once you're living in it, you'll discover that the view from the top isn't just for you. It's a vantage point from which you can light the way for others.

The Annenbergs' Wheel House Achievement at Sunnylands

Before

Walter and Leonore Annenberg were not only philanthropists but visionaries who understood that a home could be more than a private retreat. When they built Sunnylands near Palm Springs, California, in the 1960s, they envisioned a place that would nourish their lives while also catalyzing connection, diplomacy, and generosity. Rather than seeing their home as just a personal oasis, they saw it as a stage where ideas could grow, relationships could flourish, and positive change could ripple outward.

The Shift

The Annenbergs intuitively lived the Wheel House's principles. They aligned their environment with their values. Sunnylands wasn't simply luxurious; it was intentional. Designed by renowned architect A. Quincy Jones, the estate featured breathtaking gardens and art collections that reflected harmony, beauty, and purpose. Yet the true brilliance of Sunnylands was in how it served others. The Annenbergs regularly invited world leaders, cultural icons, and community members to gather there, from US presidents to British royalty. These gatherings turned their home into a hub for diplomacy, education, and the arts, extending their influence far beyond their own lives.

After (Legacy)

Today, Sunnylands continues to embody self-actualization. The estate now serves as a retreat center for international leaders, a cultural hub for art and environmental programs, and a place that inspires schoolchildren and visitors alike. The Annenbergs' vision created a home that did more than provide comfort; it actively fostered connection, beauty, and progress. In Wheel House terms, Sunnylands demonstrates the ultimate alignment—a home that supported the Annenbergs' health, joy, relationships, and purpose while becoming a vehicle for helping others.

As Walter Annenberg once said, "The greatest power is not money power, but political power." And I would agree and add that a power greater than political power is the power of love. At Sunnylands, that love was expressed through a home that continues to uplift and inspire others long after its creators are gone.

Afterword

OVERCOMING BARRIERS TO SELF

*The privilege of a lifetime is
to become who you truly are.*

—CARL JUNG

During the writing of this book, I often thought about all the people who struggle to keep adequate housing for themselves and their families. Whether they have run into hard times due to health problems, addiction, abuse, post-traumatic stress disorder (PTSD), job loss, natural disasters, acts of war, or other destructive life events, my heart goes out to them as they struggle not only to find a home but sometimes to find themselves.

While many of us who are fortunate focus on the finer characteristics of a home such as good schools for our kids, a big enough yard, or an ensuite bathroom for every bedroom, others who are less fortunate are focused on finding a home that is a safe, stable foundation for recovery or rebuilding. As an avenue for connection, counseling, and accountability, some programs offer free or reduced housing to those who need help.

Here is an example of how one person, with the help of others, found a safe and stable home that became the foundation for recovery and rebuilding.

Maya's Transformation

Before

Maya had been living in a cycle of survival for years. Addiction had taken its toll, leaving her bouncing between unstable rentals, couch-surfing, and occasionally sleeping in her car. Without a reliable place to live, the idea of focusing on treatment or steady work felt impossible. Every day was consumed by stress. *Where would she sleep tonight? Could she keep the little she owned safe?* Maya often said her life felt like a house of cards, ready to collapse at any moment.

The Shift

Through a community program, Maya was connected to transitional housing that gave her more than a roof over her head; it gave her dignity. For the first time in years she had her own room, a safe space where she could sleep through the night without fear. That stability created the foundation for her to enter addiction treatment and stick with it. With counseling and support, she began to believe in the possibility of a new chapter. Job training and career counseling soon followed, helping Maya envision a future where she wasn't just sober but thriving.

After

With a small, affordable apartment secured, Maya felt grounded enough to rebuild her life. She attended regular recovery meetings, reconnected with family, and began working part-time at a local nonprofit while completing a job-skills program. Her home became more than a shelter; it was her sanctuary—a place to rest, reflect, and grow stronger. Today, Maya points to her houseplants as proof of her progress: "If I can keep them alive, I can keep myself alive and thriving too." What once felt like an impossible climb became manageable steps that started with the stability of a home that supported her healing.

Free or reduced-cost housing while being held accountable and working a recovery program helps people rebuild their lives by providing a stable environment that removes a primary stressor and enables them to focus on their well-being. This stability allows them to engage with treatment, build a supportive social network, and develop life skills for long-term recovery.

One such program, Thistle Farms, is based in Nashville, Tennessee, with a national network of programs committed to a housing-first model for survivors. They "house up to thirty-six residents at a time in a therapeutic setting that offers healing and transformation through housing, healthcare, counseling, employment, and community building."[36] One of their slogans is "Love Heals."

I've had the pleasure of visiting Thistle Farms on many occasions. They offer great products online and in their fantastic café where I purchase closing gifts for my clients. Many graduates of the program now work at the Thistle Farms café, shop, and manufacturing facility. It gives me great joy to support Thistle Farms and other recovery programs.

Now let's look at yet another example of how housing can become the foundation of healing.

David's Transformation

Before

David, a decorated Army veteran, came home with invisible wounds. The transition to civilian life was more complicated than he expected. Crowds made him anxious, sudden noises startled him, and his small, noisy apartment near a busy road only made things worse. Sleep was scarce, and without rest, everything else—his health, his relationships, his sense of purpose—felt like they were slipping away. Though proud of his service, David often felt like a stranger in his own life.

The Shift

Then a veterans' housing program offered David a quiet home in a supportive community. It wasn't just four walls; it was a chance to breathe. With safe, peaceful surroundings and neighbors who respected his journey, David finally felt grounded enough to pursue treatment for PTSD. The stability of having a secure home gave him the courage to engage in counseling and join a peer group of other veterans who understood what he was facing.

After

In his new home, David began to rebuild his life. He created a calm space for meditation and reflection, and planted a small vegetable garden that gave him both routine and pride. Counseling and job support helped him find meaningful work with a local nonprofit that assists other veterans. For the first time in years, David slept through the night. "My home became my outpost," David said, "the base where I finally started winning battles again." His recovery didn't happen all at once, but it started the moment he had a home that felt safe.

Housing veterans after they serve their country is a passion for programs such as Zion Keepers based in Marietta, Georgia. They believe that "housing for veterans is just the first step toward a strong future, and we're here to provide the help necessary to provide safety, self-confidence, and peace of mind."[37]

A portion of the profits from the sale of this book will go to support programs such as Thistle Farms and Zion Keepers that provide housing as a first step toward healing. Many thanks to you, dear reader, for being part of the charitable support so everyone can have the opportunity to *Live in Your Wheel House*.

Acknowledgments

I'm grateful beyond measure for the extraordinary village that helped bring this book to life.

To Dan Johnston who started me on the journey to recognize myself and master the gifts that would bring me joy as I served others with them. Your ENFP cohort in Spain is where the magic started to happen.

To Jane Simmonds, my developmental editor, thank you for helping me organize my frameworks for the reader and perfect the sequence.

To the talented publishing team at StoryBuilders, thank you for believing in this message and polishing it until it shined.

To everyone at Brand Builders Group—especially my strategists Kristen Hartnagel and Larissa Salazar—thank you for your wisdom, patience, and unwavering support. And to AJ and Rory Vaden, thank you for your invaluable guidance for mission-driven messengers everywhere. What a gift to be part of a community with so much knowledge and heart.

To Terri Cole, thank you for your support and guidance. You and the fantastic group of ladies in your Flourish cohort fed my soul and provided valuable insights into codependency, boundaries, personal growth, and mental health. Terri, your calmly delivered wisdom was empowering.

To Azul Terronez and Linda Sivertsen, your feedback early in the process kept me going, encouraging me to move forward, hone my craft, and develop the frameworks. The containers you provided with other like-minded creatives were invaluable. You are both so inspiring.

To Steven Pressfield, author of *The War of Art* and so many other inspiring books for creatives, your work helped me press on and persevere through the inevitable resistance.

To Janice Renee, thank you for your feedback, your encouragement, and most of all your friendship. Your positive energy filled me up over and over again.

To my clients, past and present, thank you for trusting me with your stories and your dreams. You've taught me more than any textbook ever could about what it means to create a home that truly fits.

To Jay D'Meza who believed in me from the get-go. You inspire me with your genuine care for everyone you meet. Our Dunwoody roots served us well.

To my Sippin' Sistas and the other agents who have supported me and my mission, you know who you are. Thank you for being on this client-centered mission together.

To my Ya-Yas, thank you for the laughter and encouragement, and for always reminding me who I am when I forget.

To my family—you are my foundation and my inspiration. Everything I do begins and ends with you.

About the Author

Kim Costa is a REALTOR®, writer, speaker, and TV host whose life's work sits at the intersection of home, identity, and personal transformation. As the creator of the Live in Your Wheel House framework and founder of Lifestyle Foundations, Kim has guided countless people through one of life's most universal questions: *Does the life I'm building still fit the home I'm living in—or is something asking to change?*

Kim's journey into this work wasn't linear. It began the day she told producers of *The Oprah Winfrey Show* that they couldn't film inside her house—an instinctive moment of truth that revealed how misaligned her environment had become with the woman she was growing into. That flash of self-awareness sparked years of exploration into psychology, identity, reinvention, and the powerful ways our spaces mirror our inner lives.

Later, while Kim was writing on a soul-stirring adventure in Spain, the first threads of *Live in Your Wheel House* emerged, weaving together memoir, research, and deeply relatable stories from her work with clients who are navigating major life transitions.

A top Atlanta-area REALTOR® known for empathy, strategy, and straight talk wrapped in optimism, Kim has spent decades watching homeowners rebuild not just their kitchens or closets but their confidence, clarity, and courage.

Her signature Wheel House Method integrates the 8 Pillars of Lifestyle and the 4Ms—My Self, Mastery, Mission, and Mate(s)—to help people evaluate whether their home truly supports who they are becoming.

This simple yet transformative process has helped overwhelmed homeowners, people in transition, empty nesters, and ambitious dream-chasers find the grounding, direction, and joy they've been craving.

In addition to her real estate career, Kim is the host of *American Dream TV* and the *Live in Your Wheel House* podcast where she shares inspiring stories of home, community, and reinvention. She is also a sought-after speaker known for her heartfelt humor, practical wisdom, and ability to make audiences feel both seen and energized about what's possible next.

When she's not hosting, writing, or walking a client through a breakthrough moment, you can find her exploring the hidden gems of North Georgia and beyond—nurturing her creative spirit—or laughing through life with her two grown children or her husband, Rocky, and their extended family.

Notes

1 "America's Happiness Slump: New Report Shows U.S. in Sharp Decline," *Morningstar*, November 18, 2025, https://www.morningstar.com/news/pr-newswire/20251118ny27967/americas-happiness-slump-new-report-shows-us-in-sharp-decline.

2 Jaime Dunaway-Seale, "American Home Buyer and Seller Report: 2023 Edition," Clever, May 22, 2023, https://listwithclever.com/research/homebuyer-report-2023/.

3 Dunaway-Seale, "American Home Buyer and Seller Report: 2023 Edition."

4 https://americaathome.com/wp-content/uploads/2025/10/america-at-home-study-wave-2-download.pdf

5 Carl G. Jung, *Memories, Dreams, Reflections* (New York: Vintage, 1989).

6 C. G. Jung, *Psychological Types*, trans. Richard F. C. Hull (Princeton, NJ: Princeton University Press, 1971).

7 Isabel Briggs Myers, *MBTI Manual: A Guide to the Development and Use of the Myers-Briggs Type Indicator, Third Edition* (Consulting Psychologists Press, 1998).

8 Abraham H. Maslow, "A Theory of Human Motivation," *Psychological Review* 50, no. 4 (1943): 370–96.

9 Abraham H. Maslow, *Motivation and Personality* (New York: Harper & Row, 1954).

10 Abraham H. Maslow, *The Farther Reaches of Human Nature* (New York: Viking Press, 1971), 269.

11 Jeremy Sutton, "The Wheel of Life: How to Apply It in Coaching," *PositivePsychology*, July 29, 2020.

12 Carl R. Rogers, *On Becoming a Person: A Therapist's View of Psychotherapy* (New York: Houghton Mifflin, 1961).
13 Donald W. Winnicott, *The Maturational Processes and the Facilitating Environment: Studies in the Theory of Emotional Development* (New York: International Universities Press, 1965).
14 Marc J. Rosenberg, "Beyond Competence: It's the Journey to Mastery That Counts," Learning Solutions, The Learning Guild, May 21, 2012.
15 James Clear, "The Benefits of Mastering Your Craft," Accidental Creative, August 22, 2011.
16 Gino Wickman and Mark C. Winters. *Rocket Fuel: The One Essential Combination That Will Get You More of What You Want from Your Business* (Dallas: BenBella Books, 2016).
17 Rhett Power, "4 Reasons Why You Need a Personal Mission Statement," *Inc.*, February 19, 2016.
18 Esther Perel, *Mating in Captivity: Reconciling the Erotic and the Domestic* (New York: Harper, 2006).
19 Suzanne Degges-White, "The 13 Essential Traits of Good Friends," *Psychology Today*, March 23, 2015.
20 Yanping Li, An Pan, Dong D. Wang, et al., "Impact of Healthy Lifestyle Factors on Life Expectancies in the US Population," *Circulation* 138, no. 4 (2018): 345–55.
21 Yanping Li, et al., "Impact of Healthy Lifestyle Factors."
22 Kristen Dalli, "Adopting Healthy Habits May Make Consumers Happier, Study Finds," Consumer Affairs, September 17, 2021.
23 Gretchen Reynolds, "Set Your Exercise Goals High, but Not Too High," *The New York Times*, January 7, 2021.
24 B. J. Fogg, *Tiny Habits: The Small Changes That Change Everything* (New York: Houghton Mifflin, 2019).
25 Kim Parker, "About a Third of U.S. Workers Who Can Work from Home Now Do So All the Time," Pew Research Center, March 30, 2023.

26 Chandni Kazi and Claire Hastwell, "Remote Work Productivity Study: Surprising Findings from a 4-Year Analysis," Insights, May 20, 2025.

27 Jeffrey M. Jones, "More in U.S. Retiring, or Planning to Retire, Later," Gallup News, July 22, 2022.

28 Bronnie Ware, *The Top Five Regrets of the Dying: A Life Transformed by the Dearly Departing* (Carlsbad, CA: Hay House, 2012).

29 Barbara Hall, writer, "Northern Hospitality," *Northern Exposure*, Season 5, Episode 22, May 24, 1994.

30 Victor Cheung, "27 Feng Shui Tips to Attract Love and Improve Romance," Feng Shui Nexus, January 7, 2024.

31 Lena Abalone, "How Your Environment Affects Your Emotions," Brain World, November 20, 2021.

32 Daniel Stokols, and Ruth Barankevich, "Home Environments in an Age of Precarity," *Journal of Environmental Psychology* 99 (November 2024).

33 Clare Cooper, "The House as a Symbol of the Self," in *Designing for Human Behavior: Architecture and the Behavioral Sciences*, ed. Jon Lang et al. (Dowden, Hutchinson & Ross, 1974), 130–46.

34 Abalone, "How Your Environment Affects Your Emotions."

35 Brittany King, "Women More Likely Than Men to Have No Retirement Savings," United States Census Bureau, January 13, 2022.

36 "Our Mission," Thistle Farms. Accessed May 19, 2023, https://thistlefarms.org/pages/our-mission.

37 "A House for Every Veteran," Zion Keepers, accessed October 7, 2025, https://www.zionkeepers.org.

www.ingramcontent.com/pod-product-compliance
Lightning Source LLC
LaVergne TN
LVHW010201070526
838199LV00062B/4452